Houndini
and Other Tales

D.W. Schmidt

Copyright © 2009 by Daniel W. Schmidt.
All rights reserved.

ISBN 978-0-578-03609-0

Houndini and Other Tales

Contents

Heroes for Ghosts: an Introduction	1
Santa Rosa, 6:00 A.M.	9
The First Thanksgiving	20
Hair Today: an Expository Aside	35
Ron the Barber	38
Houndini	47
Longball	73
The World is my Urinal: a Frank Discussion	86
Boxcar Willie; Or, How I Stopped Worrying and Learned to Love the Buffet	95
Workin' Man: Odd Jobs in a State of Misery	109
Coming Home?	127
The Honking Lady: a Brief Tale of Woe and a Bundle of Joy	139
One Rider's Beginnings	149
Part 1: Forgive me, Ms. Welty	
Part 2: Where I Rode; What I Rode For	
Part 3: The Trail Less Ridden	

Before we get started:

For best results, listen to "The Apartment Song" by Tom Petty while you read this book.

Most of the pieces in this little book were drafted during the summer and fall of 2006. I was forty when I wrote this book. I am not forty any more. My employer since 1995, Holy Names University, generously granted me a sabbatical for the Fall 2006 term, which gave me the opportunity to complete this very personal project. I am indebted in many ways to our school's president, Sr. Rosemarie Nassif.

The words in these pages were written first on the cheap paper of spiral notebooks that I purchased in multipacks at the neighborhood Target store. Don't worry, I'm not offering thanks to Target. Instead, I need to give "props" to all the local fast food restaurants that served as hosts to me and my spiral notebooks. I don't know where I would be without free drink refills.

Seriously, though, folks, I am sincerely grateful to friends and family who have laughed at my jokes and stories and have encouraged me to keep writing. If you read this book, you will surely see how completely lost I would be without my beautiful and brilliant wife, Paula. I am writing this note on the eve of our twentieth anniversary, and what I realize is that I can't imagine life without her.

Finally, to my girls, Emily and Abigail, you inspire me to be better.

Heroes for Ghosts: an Introduction

I was born in a small town, Turlock, California, and I have lived most of my life within thirty miles of the hospital where I was born. The hospital isn't there anymore, or I should say the hospital moved to a new site. The old building was used for a time as an old-folks' home before it fell into disrepair and became a refuge for homeless people. It finally burned down a few years ago.

My father was an auto mechanic and my mother was a nut. I have to admit that it seems morbid to refer to my parents in the past tense, especially since they are both still alive. Though I can't exactly say my childhood was carefree, it certainly wasn't traumatic—at least not until my older brother, my only sibling, died at the age of eighteen. I was almost sixteen. Life for me, and my parents, certainly changed after his death, but this essay, and the rest of this book, is not about any of that.

As I write these words, I am forty years old, sitting at the front of a classroom while my students take an exam on *Invisible Man* and *Long Day's Journey into Night*. And this is who I am: a mildly amusing (you'll have to read on to know for sure), overweight English professor who fancies himself a writer. I teach at a very small college that calls itself a university. I know my students well. In fact, most of the kids in this Twentieth-Century American Literature class are also in my Introduction to Fiction course that met earlier today. I like my students, even the one who continues to work on her exam after everyone else has finished and left the room. Teaching, being a college professor in particular, certainly "beats workin' for a livin'," and I am good enough at it to make it look easy. I know that sounds conceited, but I have observed enough of my colleagues (at several institutions) to know that not everyone is naturally suited for the job. Fortunately, professors who can't teach often have administrative aspirations, so they get out of the classroom before they do too much harm.

I have spent the last eleven years doing what my institution has asked of me, and what has been asked of me bears little resemblance to the education and training I received in graduate school. Generally speaking, PhD programs don't prepare their degree candidates to be small-college professors. I was trained to be an "Americanist" (and I suppose I am one still), but now I'm a writing across-the-curriculum coordinator, a quasi-department chair, a supervisor of part-time instructors, and so on. Fortunately, as an MA student, I was mentored by an excellent writing teacher, Ann Krabach, who supervised graduate teaching assistants and directed the Writing Center at California State University, Stanislaus. No one ever taught me more about teaching writing.[1]

* * *

Turning forty has not been particularly difficult, but it has given me a reason to ponder. And it's been good pondering because I have discovered that I know everything I need to know. Meaning of life, relationships, spirituality, etc.—all figured out. However, I have discovered three bizarre phenomena that defy logic, reason, and everything else. I just do not understand these three things:
- The coin-operated massaging recliners they have in the shopping mall around the corner from my house.
- Butt-crack tattoos.
- Fantasy football leagues.

---

[1] My wife, who is a composition expert, was also mentored by Ann and now has her old job as Director of the Writing Center at CSUS.

Let's start with the message chairs. At our local mall, they are located just a few feet away from the Dairy Queen-Orange Julius and across the way from Macy's. These chairs seem so wrong in so many ways. Do the people who own the chairs (perhaps it's the company that manages the mall) imagine that some tired fellow might say to his wife, "Mildred, I'm not going with you into that Macy's store unless I can sit here in this chair and shake a little while. Now give me some quarters"? I am pleased, and relieved quite frankly, to report that I have never seen anyone getting an automated massage in those chairs, but I have seen many little kids with ice cream cones in their hands climbing around on them.

Don't kid yourself. I understand the idea behind the all-too-popular[2] butt-crack tattoo. When combined with less than modest clothing and a certain kind of underwear, the crack "tat" could be seen as sexy. I just cannot imagine how any self-respecting person could bring herself (it's usually a she) to get into the position necessary to have the tattoo applied to that part of her person.

Finally, I played football in high school. I still enjoy watching football. I have also enjoyed a number of fantasies in my forty years. None has ever involved football.

---

[2] I was going to use the word "ubiquitous" instead of "all-too-popular." Ubiquitous would have been less wordy, but I'm sick of seeing the word ubiquitous everywhere. I am also tired of these words: bundle, amazing, and intangible.

* * *

Most of the incidents and experiences described in this book happened more than a dozen years ago, though in some cases the "story" has been in my head since the actual event. I suppose the real result of turning forty has been a new resolve to tell these "true stories"—to distill the memory for me (and my wife, and even our kids—who make only brief appearances in these pages). The mostly narrative essays included here cover (with a few exceptions) a period of about five years—from 1989 (when my wife and I got married) to 1994 (the year our first child, Emily, was born). There are lots of reasons why this particular time period will remain stuck in my head until I write out some of the memories. Besides getting married and starting a family, my wife and I moved from California to Illinois, then to Missouri, and finally back to California. We went to graduate school (she earned an MA, while I got my PhD) at Southern Illinois University at Carbondale, took out massive school loans,[3] and then struggled to find real jobs. So obviously I'm talking about a pivotal period in my life. On the other hand, it's funny that a disillusioned (dare I say "burned out") academic like

---

[3] The federal student loan program is quite generous in loaning money to married graduate students—or at least they were in the late 1980s and early '90s. I don't know what the situation is now. I just hope we can pay off our student loans before we want to retire. I have given up on the idea that the loans would be amortized before our kids go to college. I've never used the word "amortize" in a sentence. I hope I used it correctly.

me would write a batch of narrative essays about the time when I was actively and ambitiously striving to become a member of academia. But these pieces are about the real people and real places (and a few animals) we encountered during those years.

The truth is I have only one decent story, the "Pigeon Story," from graduate school that I still tell today. When the weather warms up, my students sometimes ask if we can have class outside. This request is not unreasonable on their part because the building that houses my office and the classrooms in which I teach has no air conditioning. Since our college is located in the San Francisco Bay Area, the lack of air conditioning (or even ventilation) is not usually a problem. However, on the uncommon occasions when the temperature nears eighty degrees, the classrooms, especially late in the afternoon, become totally bereft of fresh air. So inevitably someone will say, "Can we have class outside today?" I respond by telling the "Pigeon Story." It's not much of a story, but I'll let the reader decide.

Faner Hall, where most English classes were taught at SIUC, is a long, four-story concrete building. Quite often in the spring a burst of hot humid weather would hit southern Illinois before the cooling system in Faner was turned on for the season. The damp heat turned Faner into a sweatbox. One day, Professor John Howell, a somewhat old-fashioned Americanist who taught me everything I know about Faulkner, decided to let our American poetry class meet outside the steamy classroom in one of the building's courtyards. Well, anyway, we were all spread out in the courtyard, sitting on metal patio furniture, when a pigeon swooped down ("out of nowhere"), skimmed Dr. Howell's perfectly combed salt and pepper hair, and crashed on the patio table John was using for his books and notes. The pigeon quickly recovered from his accident (?) and disappeared somewhere in a nook of one of the upper floors. Incredibly, no one laughed, chuckled, or guffawed. We sat stunned as John resumed talking after a short pause.

So the pigeon did not really disturb the class. He just destroyed it. For the rest of the term, no one in the class could shake the image of the dive-bombing pigeon. It hung about our necks as we tried to decode the meanings of the modernists and cringed at the confessions of the Beats. And the bird hovered above every before- and after-class discussion, ready to interrupt any conversation that lasted more than a moment:

"Did you do the reading?"

"Most of it. Have you started your paper yet?"

"No. What do you suppose was the deal with that pigeon?"

And that was that, no more talk of poetry or assignments. If I learned nothing else from that class, I realized I would never take a class out of doors.

* * *

I am sitting now in front of another class (but in the same classroom as before). This time it's a second-semester freshman-writing course. The students are supposed to be helping each other with their drafts. There is a student in this class who recently sent me an email that read

> Dr. Schmidt is me Justine L. I[4] have the conference with you at 11:00 but im really sick can I just email you my essay.

God help me and Justine. And God help anyone who reads the rest of this book.

---

[4] This "I" and the next one were typed by the student in the lower case, but the damned Word program won't let me type the lower-case I by itself.

Santa Rosa, 6:00 A.M.

My wife, Paula, is an intelligent, funny, organized, and responsible woman. I, on the other hand, am good at Trivial Pursuit. So, looking back, I can understand why there was considerable hand wringing and gnashing of teeth among her family and friends when we announced our engagement on Christmas Eve, 1988. It didn't help that we had just met in September. On my family's side, there was simply a feeling of relief that at the ripe old age of 23 I had convinced a woman, any woman, to marry me. We enjoyed a whirlwind albeit low budget romance. It began virtually the day we met in the Writing Center at CSU, Stanislaus in Turlock, California. I was a graduate student working in the Writing Center, and Paula was the Center's secretary.⁵ Our first "date" was an Amnesty International concert at the Oakland-Alameda County Coliseum, where we saw Bruce Springsteen perform on his 38th birthday.⁶ Paula insists I put date in quotation marks because (1) she had to pay for her own ticket and (2) my friend, Mike, went to the show with us. By Thanksgiving, we were talking about marriage. And early in the morning on Christmas Eve, we drove into the Sierra Foothills to the historic gold rush town of Columbia, a California State Park.⁷ After breakfast in the Columbia House Restaurant, I gave her the engagement ring we had already picked out together, and I asked her to marry me.

We were married on July 15, 1989 in my parents' backyard. They had bought the house just a few months before I met Paula. It was a big house that needed some work, and it had a large, beautiful backyard that could accommodate our 150 guests. We spent the months leading up to the wedding getting the house and yard ready, and a year and a half later my parents divorced and the house was sold.⁸

---

⁵ For those readers not familiar with the term "secretary," it means literally "administrative assistant."

⁶ I believe Bruce, the world's greatest rocker, had recently broken up with his first wife.

⁷ A trip to Columbia at Christmastime has become a family tradition. Our kids look forward to visiting the old-time businesses on Columbia's main street: the candy store, the toy store, the blacksmith, etc.

⁸ The house was bought by mysterious people who immediately turned it into a compound. Trees, bushes, and chained gates were used to keep out unwanted guests and prevent even passersby from seeing through the perimeter of the property. The people may be pot growers or meth cookers, but they've maintained their jungle-like façade for more than 15 years.

It was a beautiful wedding, probably the best wedding I've ever seen. We have the pictures to prove it (but no video, someone forgot to push the record button). The days leading up to the wedding were, of course, hectic, and we dealt with the typical squabbles between the various parties involved: bride, groom, groom's parents, bride's mother, bride's aunts, uncles, cousins, grandparents, etc. My memory here may not be completely accurate—but if I remember correctly—I was probably the cause of most of the trouble. Now I'm not saying I was a jerk or that I was purposely giving the others grief. It's just that in the spring of 1989, I was a very busy boy. In addition to the wedding preparations (actually I did little—except for the yard work) and the pre-marital counseling, all I was doing was finishing my coursework for my MA, completing a thesis on Hemingway's Nick Adams stories, trying to get into a PhD program, teaching developmental writing, and playing first base for a very competitive slow-pitch softball team.[9] In my defense, I had about a 20-game hitting streak that spring, and I hit about .750.

A few months before the wedding, my future mother-in-law and one of Paula's aunts from her dad's side came out to the house on a Saturday to plan decorations and seating arrangements and so on. Unfortunately, my plans for the weekend included writing a

---

[9] I played with my cousin Rodney on this team, which consisted of five or six Portuguese brothers, my cousin, a few of his friends from high school, and me.

thesis chapter and playing in a softball tournament. Between games, I was writing in the basement office of the house, and I didn't give the visitors the attention they expected. However, like the lady said, "Attention must be paid." But I didn't pay it, and boy did I pay for it.[10] I swear it was not an intentional snub. A snub, though, is a snub, and it hurt Paula's feelings that I had made such a bad impression.

    We endured, though. In May, Paula graduated with her BA, and I finished the MA. After the wedding, we honeymooned for a week in Ashland, Oregon, and two weeks after that we began our new life together by moving from California to southern Illinois—where I would earn by PhD and Paula her MA. I sold my car, a 1983 Nissan Sentra, to pay for a one-way rental truck to haul our stuff (mostly hand-me-down furniture, our books, and clothes) across the country. Paula had a 1986 Dodge Colt, which we would keep until we sold it to pay for another rental truck four years later when we moved back to California. Our second vehicle would be an old Puch moped that Paula's Uncle Bob sold to us for $50. Paula's other uncle, Warren, had a tow dolly that would allow us to tow the Colt behind the rental truck. The deal was that we could use the tow dolly for our trip and then when we got to Illinois I would sell it and send the money back to Warren. The plan worked

---

[10] Interestingly, Linda Loman says this line in <u>Death of a Salesman</u>, and my mother-in-law's name is Lynda, and Paula's aunt is named Linda.

great—except the part about selling the thing. It took about two months to find an old farmer to buy it, and then he didn't exactly want to pay top dollar for it. While I was trying to sell it, the dolly had to sit in an overflow parking lot at the married-student housing complex, Evergreen Terrace, and the staff were not too happy with the arrangement. But I'm getting ahead of the story.

Our eastward migration began on a hot Saturday afternoon. The family brain trust (my dad and Paula's uncles) decided we would be better off to leave later in the day in order to avoid the heat and traffic of the daytime. We would drive through the desert regions of California at night and try to make it as far across Arizona as we could before we stopped at a motel. Our route began in Modesto on Highway 99. We drove south on 99 to Bakersfield. At Bakersfield we took Highway 58 across the Tehachapi mountains, through Mojave to Barstow, where we met Interstate 40, which we followed east through Arizona, New Mexico, Texas, and into Oklahoma. In Oklahoma City, we switched to I-44, which took us to St. Louis and the mighty Mississippi. This route, of course, follows the path of old Route 66, the Mother Road, and our journey essentially reversed the one many of our family members had taken years before as they came to California from places like Oklahoma, Texas, and Arkansas.

After we said our tearful goodbyes and headed out on the highway, I thought of my favorite passage from *The Grapes of*

Wrath. Early in the book, as the Joads begin their trip in their old Hudson Super Six, Al Joad asks his mother,

"Got any hills 'tween here an' California, Ma?"

Ma replies, "Seems to me they's hills. . .'Course I dunno."
The Joads' ignorance is at once humorous and terrifying. The reader can stop right there in the novel. This conversation tells us everything we need to know about where the book is going and how the journey is going to turn out for this sad family.

Fortunately for Paula and me, we were not as geographically unaware as the Joads. And we had the invaluable assistance of the AAA Trip-Tik. I do not know if AAA still offers the Trip-Tik service now that we live in the age of GPS and Mapquest, but in the old days a AAA member could go to a local branch office and have AAA work out the best route for any given road trip. The actual Trip-Tik was a narrow notebook with the spiral binding at the top, like a steno-pad. Each page was a section of map that guided the traveler along the route and showed where each junction and change in direction would occur. Even though we had looked over the entire route on the map and we knew which highways we would take, it was comforting (especially since we were driving a truck and towing a vehicle) to have the Trip-Tik there to highlight each portion of the trip.

We traveled into the night over the Tehachapi Pass and into the desert, past places like Borax, Twenty-mule Team Road, and

Edward's Air Force Base. I do not remember what time it was when we reached Barstow, but I do recall that we had to work our way through road construction and detours to meet up with I-40. We got onto I-40, double checked Trip-Tik, and decided that we would definitely need to get fuel in Needles. Just after we passed the last exits and services for the Barstow area, we came upon a road sign that told us Needles was a mere 210 MILES (!!) away. We were now having our own Joad moment. As I said, we had just checked the Trip-Tik, which told us that Needles was about 100 miles down the road. Another examination of the Trip-Tik booklet revealed that there was one page, one very crucial page when you're in the desert at night, missing.[11]

The upshot of this slight miscalculation was this: there were no services between where we were and Needles, and I didn't have enough fuel to go 210 MILES (!!). We had to go back to Barstow for fuel, but there weren't a lot of available exits and entrances to the freeway out there in the middle of nowhere/hell. If I were not behind the wheel of a large moving van with a vehicle attached, I might have been tempted to do something illegal and just cut across the median to the westbound side of the freeway. About ten miles down the road we found an exit, where someone had apparently attempted an outpost but failed, and we turned the rig around and

---

[11] At this juncture it seems fair to point out that California is one hell of a big state. From Modesto to the Arizona border on I-40 is well over 600 miles; it's 800 miles from the Oregon border to the Mexico.

headed back to Barstow. We avoided disaster, but our confidence in the drive-by-night plan was a bit shaken. As we re-traced our path toward Needles, I was filled with both apprehension and anger (I still wonder if the AAA employee who prepared the Trip-Tik left the page out as a prank).

Determined to make up for lost time, I resolved to drive for as long as I possibly could. As we crossed the border and passed through Kingman, the Arizona night began to be punctuated by spectacular lightning strikes. The crooked exclamation points would light up miles and miles of the surreal high desert landscape for an instant, and then the all-encompassing darkness would envelop us again. The light show continued for the rest of the night—through the high country of Flagstaff and east to the New Mexico border. We drove straight through Arizona, stopping only for fuel.[12]

We finally stopped to sleep in Gallup, New Mexico. We checked into a Super 8 (or maybe it was a Best Western) at about noon, jumped in their pool to unwind from the road, and then hit the hay. We slept only until the wee hours of the morning, so that we could get back on the road. We passed through Albuquerque while the city slept and pressed on toward Texas. As the endless horizon

---

[12] In our travels back and forth across the southwest, we always found the Love's Country Stores to be the most consistent and reliable places to stop for gas, snacks, and my large fountain drinks. The best truck stop on I-40, though, is the Giant Truck Stop, which sits practically on the Continental Divide, between Gallup and Grants, New Mexico. It's a Truck Stop/Small Town where the traveler can find just about anything. For an old-time roadside experience, the traveler should stop once at a Stuckey's. Once should do the trick.

and the stark but beautiful red rock and dirt began to reappear, I became hungry. I exited the freeway at a little town called Santa Rosa. Although we would settle for about anything, we were hoping to find a café where we could get a real breakfast—like a Denny's Grand Slam. What we found was that the town was closed. There indeed was a café, but it didn't open until 6:00 A.M. We would have to wait in the truck 15 or 20 minutes before we could get our breakfast. We figured we could wait. There was no sense wasting a stop only to have to stop again a little ways down the road.

We sat down in a booth in the café, and a sleepy waitress handed us menus. We looked for something cheap and both settled on the "Hotcakes and Ham (or Sausage)." When the waitress brought our orders, everything looked okay. There was nothing special about the ham. Each of us got one thick slice of the deli-style processed ham. The hotcakes, for their part, were thick and golden brown. We applied butter and then maple syrup. The syrup soon disappeared, and I thought to myself, "These cakes are thick!" I gave them more syrup and began to eat. But it was no use. I couldn't get anywhere with those cakes. I bit and chewed and put more syrup on them. I looked down and it was like the loaves and the fishes. There seemed to be as much there as when I started. Finally, Paula said what I was just beginning to realize:

"These aren't pancakes."

"The menu said 'hotcakes.'"

"Well, they're hotcakes made from corn flour."

"They are quite absorbent—and filling. Have you ever heard of making pancakes, er--hotcakes, from corn?"

"My people call it 'maize.'"[13]

"Welcome to New Mexico. You know, I like corn bread. I really like it."

"Yeah."

"But I can't eat this."

"Nope. Just eat the ham, and let's get back on the road."[14]

So we moved on. But this story ends here in Santa Rosa. Yes, we had hundreds of miles to go and other obstacles to overcome before we would settle into our apartment in Carbondale, Illinois. Somehow, though, the memory of that first trip (and everything that led to it) concludes with Santa Rosa and the corn pancakes. The disappearing syrup is the particular and enduring

---

[13] Paula didn't actually say this line. In fact, when she read this line soon after I wrote it, she said she doesn't even remember the old TV commercial for Mazola corn oil, which featured a young indigenous-looking woman walking through a cornfield. I think her first line was "Corn—my people call it 'maize.'" I just thought it might be funny at this point in the conversation. However, I realize now that for some readers a falsehood of this nature calls into question the veracity of everything I have said and might say. I also realize that readers might object to an off-hand reference to what was probably an insensitive caricature. I would just like to say that I am really, really, sorry.

[14] A few years after this incident we learned about "hoe cakes" during a visit to the Silver Dollar City amusement park outside of Branson, Missouri. In the pioneer days, a poor farmer or farm worker would take corn meal and water (maybe it was milk) with him out to the field. At lunchtime, the individual made a fire, cleaned off his hoe blade, mixed his corn and liquid into a paste or batter, and then poured it onto the hoe blade. The hoe cake was cooked over the open fire with the cook flipping the cake several times to insure that it would cook evenly.

image that stands for the whole, and I realize now in the writing of it that this incident marked the end of our courtship (which included the wedding and the honeymoon) and the beginning of the crazy love affair/journey that would be our life together.

The First Thanksgiving

B esides the availability of cheap real estate, I see no good reason to live in the lower Midwest. On the day we arrived in Illinois the temperature was in the low-nineties and so was the humidity. When I climbed out of the Budget truck, I felt like I had died and gone to the sauna. The sky was hazy in a way I had never seen. It was not smoggy like California gets sometimes, but it was a vague off-white that I soon learned passed for "sunny" in those parts at that time of the year. The heat and humidity weren't just stifling after driving all day in the air-conditioned rental truck; I felt almost paralyzed. And then I saw people, apparently insane, engaged in outdoor physical activity.

When we pulled into the married student housing complex (Evergreen Terrace), I parked the truck in the small parking lot next to the building that housed our apartment. Our building was near the front of the complex, and, thus, near the office. Adjacent to the office were recreation facilities including a playground and an outdoor basketball court. As I struggled to breathe in the hot, wet air, I noticed that children were playing in the playground, and there was a fairly intense, full-court pick-up game being played on the basketball court. My mind, nay, my entire body, could not comprehend how these young boys and men could run up and down the asphalt court, jump, shoot, pass, and call out to each other. I found that just trying to concentrate on an idea or upcoming task made me sweat profusely.

Amazingly, in just a few short months, this same playground would be covered in a blanket of snow. And instead of sitting in an air-conditioned truck cab, Paula and I would be sitting in an airplane, an L1011, on a runway at the St. Louis airport, waiting for the wings to be de-iced and the freezing baggage handlers to finish loading the plane. Our family all pitched in on airfare so we could come home for Christmas. We wanted to spend time with the folks at home, but I think mostly we wanted to escape the single-digit temperatures we encountered our first December in Illinois. Even though we didn't know it at the time, those first four months, from our arrival to our Christmas vacation, exposed us to the three seasons of the Heartland climate: Muggy, Freezing, and Autumn. Of the three, only autumn (which didn't last very long) is what I would call comfortable. In the fall, the air is drier and the temperature tends to be moderate.[15]

* * *

Our first Illinois fall was a difficult time, especially for Paula. First and foremost, she had to deal with the stunning revelation that she had married a complete idiot. This sad realization probably began as we rolled across the bridge into Illinois. We (I) decided to take Route 3 south along the river through Red Bud and Chester to Route 149 east and then Route 13 at Murphysboro to Carbondale.[16] This way turned out to be the scenic route, which of course meant that the views were beautiful and that it took an hour longer that any of the other routes.[17] The length of the last leg of our journey would not have mattered much,

---

[15] I remember that when I met the Chair of the SIU English Department, Dr. Richard Peterson, he told a group of us (graduate students) that a popular local saying was "If you don't like the weather, wait a minute." I have since learned that other regions of the country have similar sayings. These areas tend to be places where the weather is usually crappy. And when the weather changes, it's most often not for the better.

[16] This was the last decision I was ever allowed to make.

[17] In my defense, we discovered that, although one can take a half-dozen different routes, there is no good or quick way to get from St. Louis to Carbondale. Three years later, when I "commuted" from Springfield, MO to Carbondale every week for one semester, I settled on taking I-64 from St. Louis to Route 127 south near Nashville to Route 13 at Murphysboro and then east to Carbondale.

except that we needed to reach the Evergreen Terrace office before it closed at 3:00 p.m. We pulled into town about 2:45. And then we (I) couldn't find the 25,000-student university in a town of the same size. If we couldn't find the housing complex by 3:00, we would be forced to spend another night in a motel, which we really could not afford. So, our two thousand-mile trip had come down to a fifteen-minute window of opportunity to locate our new home, and the tension inside the truck cab increased with every passing minute.

Finally, as we reached the intersection of Route 13 and Route 51, we saw a small sign for SIU. We turned right (South) on 51 and found the university. We entered the grounds of the school in the rental truck (with the Dodge Colt in tow) and followed the main loop to the left, hoping to see a sign for Evergreen Terrace or married student housing. We found that the campus is quite large and scenic as we wound around buildings and ponds and through wooded areas. Eventually, we came to a drive that departed from the main loop and promised to lead toward Evergreen Terrace. This drive brought us out to a main road, W. Pleasant Hill Road.[18] Across the road was the housing complex. We walked (sweating) into the office at about 2:58. We were given the keys to Apartment 177-7, which, as I said before, was at the front of the complex—near the entrance and the office. 177-7 was an upstairs apartment, and I

---

[18] If we had simply stayed on 51 south, in about a mile it would have lead to Pleasant Hill Road, where we could have turned right and traveled about one-half mile to Evergreen Terrace.

immediately began looking forward to carrying my parents' old sofa and loveseat up the flight of stairs.

We knew unloading the truck and moving everything into the apartment would be a strenuous job for the two of us. But the steamy weather made the task downright hellish. We quickly made a plan: as soon as I disconnected the Colt from the truck and tow dolly, Paula would go to town to get groceries, drinks, and ice (as we had none of these things)—while I began unloading.[19] What happened next was perhaps my biggest screw-up ever and definitely the only Incredible Hulk moment of my life. I set about freeing the Colt, and I started by disconnecting the trailer wiring between the tow dolly and the truck. And then, maybe because I was already delirious from the humidity or because I was still frazzled from our frantic search for the apartment complex, I released the latch on top of the tow dolly's tongue that locks it onto the ball of the truck's hitch. The weight of the car on the tow dolly instantly lifted the tongue a foot in the air above the ball. And the whole car-tow dolly unit began to roll back, away from the truck.

At some level, but probably not a conscious one, I immediately recognized two important facts: (1) I would never get the car off the tow dolly unless the dolly was re-connected to the

---

[19] This trip to the store was the first of several in which, due to a lack of funds and income, the purchase of groceries would be made with a credit card. We were not using the card to earn frequent flier miles or cash rebates; we were broke, and we had to dig a bigger hole in order to eat and drink.

truck's hitch, and (2) I was on my own (Paula was up in the apartment). I don't think I turned green as I grabbed the tongue of the dolly, squatted down, thrust forward, and just plain willed the damned thing back on the ball, but it may have been the closest I've come to pure, blind rage. I then safely unhooked the car's front wheels and backed the Colt off the dolly. I disconnected the tongue from the ball (again) and wheeled the dolly out of the way. When Paula came out to get in the car, I explained what had just happened. I think she laughed (thanks to the little drama's happy ending). But as she drove away, I can't imagine that she was brimming with confidence in her new idiot-husband, and she had to think twice about actually returning from the store.

I began to work and sweat profusely. After one trip up the stairs, I rummaged through the truck and found some Styrofoam cups. I filled the two cups with water from the kitchen sink and placed them both in the freezer. When I came upstairs with the next load, I drank the contents of one cup and refilled it. The trip after that I drank the other one. I repeated this process until Paula returned with ice and drinks.[20]

* * *

---

[20] I should also note that after about the third trip I was wearing only a pair of shorts and tennis shoes. I wouldn't be so bold today, given my advanced weight, but at the time I was in decent shape (about 180 lbs.). The reader might like to know that the following words have never been used to describe me: skinny, thin, and slim.

Besides learning to live with a moron, Paula had to spend that first fall working in a local photocopying business. I've said elsewhere that Paula and I went to Illinois for graduate school, so that she could get an MA and I could do the PhD. That's exactly what happened, but it wasn't the initial plan. Paula had not applied to the SIU MA program when we got married. We made the decision to move to Illinois because SIU had accepted me into their doctoral program and offered me an assistantship that would allow me to teach a few classes for a small salary and get a break on out-of-state tuition. Paula's undergraduate degree was in Liberal Studies, with a concentration in English. In California, a person who wants to teach elementary school majors in Liberal Studies before entering a post-BA credential program. We figured that Paula, with her Liberal Studies degree, would be able to work as a substitute to begin with and then possibly become certified to teach in Illinois. But one should never underestimate the lunacy of state, local, and educational bureaucracies. Paula discovered that no person with any connection to education in the great state of Illinois had ever heard of a "Liberal Studies" major.

Apparently, in Illinois, undergraduates who want to become elementary school teachers major in something called "Elementary

Education."[21] This fundamental difference between California and Illinois forced Paula to seek an alternate form of employment. As I mentioned in the previous story, Paula's an intelligent, organized, and personable woman, so she has always been good at getting hired. She found work at the Copy Shop, a business that made photocopies, flyers, pamphlets, and "course packs" for instructors at the university. Paula was a particularly valuable employee because she was adept at working with Pagemaker, the computer graphics program that the store used for most of its documents. The store's staff consisted of the owner, a man whose name I have forgotten but I'll call him Larry, a bossy woman named Donna, a young woman named Anna Emanus, and Paula.[22] Anna and her husband Doug quickly became our best friends in Carbondale. We did just about everything together for the next three years. When we moved to Springfield, Missouri for Paula's job at Southwest Missouri State University and I had to make a weekly commute to Carbondale, I slept in their spare room every Tuesday and Wednesday night for 15 weeks.

---

[21] I would have to do some further research, but I suspect that this "Elementary Education" major is similar to what we in California call "Liberal Studies."
[22] There is nothing remarkable or interesting to say about Larry, except that he once told Anna and Paula that he had grown up in a small, rural Illinois town and he never saw an African-American in person until he was 18 years old.

Some people have the friends that you would expect them to have—not us.[23] Doug Emanus was (is) an Illinois native and a Republican. Doug and I are about the same age (and same size, too), but when we met he was an undergraduate at SIU studying Electrical Engineering.[24] He met Anna while they were both in the U.S. Navy. Anna, on the other hand, was a funny and wiry little gal from Texas. She was a dedicated smoker, and she was, as my own Texas-born relatives would say, a pip. We bowled together at the university student center, went to see movies at the old discount theater in Murphysboro, and tried out all sorts of restaurants, cafes, roadhouses, and a few bars in the tri-state area.[25] Doug and I played softball together and took up golf at the same time. Mostly, though, we just had a lot of laughs and enjoyed each other's company.

What I loved about Doug and Anna was the way they yelled at each other—often. In my own (still new) marriage the question of who was in charge had been settled the day I prematurely unhitched

---

[23] Our best friends today, Mike and Linda Simpson, whom we met at church, are about 12 years older than we are. Mike, whose ethnic background is best described as mixed, was a butcher his entire adult life before "retiring" and getting a new job as a maintenance manager. Linda, who is a cancer survivor, works as an office manager for a firm that operates assisted-living facilities.

[24] The only thing Engineering and English have in common is that they are often listed one after the other alphabetically.

[25] Our most memorable and miserable dining experience occurred at a place called the Acapulco Café (not affiliated with the Acapulco restaurant chain). The lower Midwest is great for buffets, catfish, and barbeque—but not Mexican food. So someone decided to try a Mexican restaurant in Murphysboro. It was not a successful experiment. They did succeed, however, in devising a way to make refried beans taste like Palmolive dishwashing soap.

the tow dolly (maybe even before that), but for the Emani (we decided this should be the plural of Emanus) the matter was still subject to heated debate and negotiation. In order to keep things fair, stuff like household duties, chores, and responsibilities were assigned, re-assigned, and regularly traded. This arrangement naturally led to disagreements about whose turn it was, say, to wash the dishes or take out the trash. The ensuing debate would take five or ten minutes as the terms of the current arrangement were reviewed. At first, I thought it would be impossible for these two people to coexist in a long-term relationship, but eventually I realized that these squabbles were not serious. Anna and Doug just worked out their relationship in this seemingly combative way. We haven't seen the Emani in about thirteen or fourteen years, but Paula and Anna exchange Christmas cards. They obviously could stay together, and they've raised a beautiful family (judging from the pictures in the Christmas cards).

* * *

Neither Paula nor Anna worked for very long at the Copy Shop. Anna got a job at a local legal office, where she worked until Doug finished his degree and they moved to Texas. For Paula, being forced to work for Larry at the Copy Shop changed her life. If she had been allowed to begin teaching elementary school in

Illinois, she might still be doing that today. Instead, that first fall she met some of the people from the SIU English Department and learned about the various options within the MA program, and she realized she was interested in the teaching of writing. So Paula applied for admission to the graduate program, and (thanks to a bit of finagling by the program director, Dr. Hans Rudnick) she was awarded an assistantship—which allowed her to begin teaching in the spring of 1990. "And that," as Robert Frost said, "has made all the difference." Paula finished her MA in English, with a concentration in Rhetoric and Composition, in 1992. Her thesis dealt with the impact a university writing center can have on students' writing and their attitudes toward writing, and it helped qualify her for her current position as Director of the Writing Center at CSU, Stanislaus.[26] But I have gotten way ahead of the story, again.

Of course, we couldn't see beyond the last few months of 1989. We could see, though, that we were really on our own, and we had to depend on each other.[27] I know that may sound too cliché and too Oprah for many readers. In retrospect, I think our marriage benefited immensely from our situation, and I know it's a stronger

---

[26] I can't begin to describe what Paula's career has meant to me. Having both of us in the business has probably kept me in it.

[27] Other things I remember seeing that fall were (1) the Loma Prieta earthquake back home, which interrupted the World Series (Athletics versus Giants) Bay Area fans had waited decades to see, and (2) Tom Petty and the Heartbreakers, who played the SIU Arena on their Full Moon Fever tour.

relationship today because of it. Still, we weren't looking forward to spending the holidays away from our families. Fortunately, the folks back home eliminated the possibility of spending Christmas break in Illinois. Thanksgiving, though, was another matter.

For my dysfunctional family and me, holidays (Thanksgiving especially) were days simply to be endured since my brother's death in 1981. Paula's family, while no less dysfunctional, really shape their lives around holidays, and Thanksgiving is in many ways their biggest event of the year.[28] Thanksgiving for them (us) is not a single day to eat excessively. Instead, the holiday is a weekend-long family reunion that happens at a place we call "the property." The property is a remote piece of land located in the Sierra foothills not far--as the crow flies--from Yosemite National Park. I'll talk at greater length about the property in later stories, but in a nutshell the place is a kind of hillbilly heaven, complete with old trailers, where several branches of the clan gather to ride dirt bikes and all-terrain vehicles. Thanksgiving 1989 would be the first time since she was a little kid that Paula had not spent the holiday with her family in the hills.

---

[28] Paula's Grandma Bea, who was one of the sweetest human beings who ever lived, was born on the fourth of July, and she liked nothing better than having her entire family together on holidays. Grandma Bea was born in Arkansas, and she lived a *Grapes of Wrath* childhood. As matriarch of the family (she was widowed in the early 1970s), she fought against the transience and fragmentation of modern life.

The sun came up on a beautiful Thanksgiving Day in Carbondale. We had decided that we wouldn't try to cook a Thanksgiving dinner for ourselves, so we made plans to go to a restaurant in a little town north of Carbondale called Johnston City. I don't remember the name of the restaurant, but I'll call it Larry's Place. Larry's Place, which had run advertisements in the newspaper for their home-style holiday dinner, was like most of the locally owned eating establishments in the heartland. It was in an old building on a rural road, and, even though it was not billed as such, it had the look and feel of a roadhouse.

We arrived at Larry's just after noon, only to discover that the place was already busy. It seems to me that I had made a reservation a few days before, but nonetheless we had to wait in the lounge for at least an hour before getting a table. In the lounge we watched the NFL game on TV, and we noticed that most of the other parties waiting there were families who had swung by the old folks' home to pick up grandma and/or grandpa before coming to Larry's Place. When we were finally seated, we were given a large, round table, big enough for five or six people. While the table allowed us to have plenty of room for our turkey dinner with all the fixings, the whole dining experience was more or less dismal. And I think we felt silly sitting there—just the two of us—at the big table, while other families tried to make room for grandma or grandpa's wheelchair at their own tables.

After we ate, we headed back to Carbondale. It really was a beautiful day—maybe the best weather we had seen since moving to Illinois. It was a day perfect for raking leaves and playing football in the yard. We went to the empty campus and took some pictures of the place to send home to the friends and family. We took pictures of each other in front of a number of the old brick buildings, and we snapped photos of the red squirrels that were common on the SIU campus but non-existent in California. The pictures took about one-half hour, and then we started back to the apartment. I decided it was time for a soda, so on the way home I stopped by the only open store, a twenty-four-hour convenience store that was called "24-Hour Convenience Mart."[29] When I entered the store, I was taken aback by the appearance of the store clerk. She was an African-American woman with what I can only describe as a man face. The clerk was a man-faced woman who was apparently angry (probably rightly so) to be working in a place like 24-Hour Convenience Mart on Thanksgiving. I avoided eye contact with the clerk and walked to the back part of the store and the fountain drink machine. I filled up a thirty-two-ounce cup with ice and Diet Pepsi, put a lid on it, and slid in a straw. I returned to the front counter and paid for my drink without really talking to the man-faced woman. But as I put my change in my pocket and picked up the cup off the

---

[29] I have as yet failed to mention that some people think I have a serious addiction to diet soda.

counter, I looked directly at the woman and said, "Happy Thanksgiving."

The woman's face was instantly and miraculously transformed. I was suddenly looking at a completely different person. She smiled kindly (perhaps gratefully) and said, "Happy Thanksgiving to you." I walked out of the store feeling a little happier than when I went in. I explained to Paula what had happened inside the store, just as I have related the experience here, and we went back to the apartment. I don't want to portray this little episode as some great convenience-store epiphany that made the lonely holiday (and living in Carbondale) more bearable, nor am I saying that my off-hand courtesy was a "good deed" that brightened the woman's day. In fact, I have no idea what happened next to her. The convenience store was about a half-mile from Evergreen Terrace, and I went in there many times over the next three years (even after we moved a few miles away). But I never saw the man-faced woman again.

Hair Today: An Expository Aside

[Author's note: this piece can be read either before or after "Ron the Barber," which follows in the text. Strictly speaking, this essay does not fit in the overall narrative "flow" or the timeframe of the book. It exists in our time, the present moment, and it is included here because it shows that many of the issues described in "Ron the Barber" remain unresolved. One might call it a very long footnote with footnotes of its own.]

I have an enormous head. I have the XL and XXL hats, baseball caps, and helmets to prove it. When I played football in high school, I could be sure that I would get a helmet that had not been previously worn by anyone except my older brother.[30] If an average grown man tries on one of my baseball caps, he looks like a little child playing dress-up. He can tap the bill of the cap and it will spin easily and freely around his head. If we are out riding

---

[30] It's safe to say that the big head runs in the Schmidt family. My brother was nearly a perfect size 8, my dad is a 7½, and I'm about a 7 ¾.

motorcycles and ATVs and a guest needs to borrow a helmet, I usually caution against using mine because the rider almost always looks like one of those bobble-head dolls with my helmet on, and I don't think that that is going to provide effective protection.

People with small heads have no idea what it is like to walk around with a watermelon on top of your shoulders. For instance, the size of my head puts an incredible amount of pressure on my hair. Now, I'm not saying that it puts actual physical pressure on my hair follicles. What I mean is that the size of my head forces me to be very careful in selecting a hairstyle. Any kind of buzz or crew cut is out of the question.[31] And it is absolutely imperative that I never go bald. If I ever go bald, I might have to have three round dots tattooed in a triangular formation on the back of my head with the words "Brunswick" printed below. Luckily, I've always had a good head of hair, but I am becoming increasingly worried about my forehead. It's definitely getting bigger. Recently, I was at our

---

[31] A few years ago, my wife, Paula, and her sister decided I should have a "summer cut"—like the one given to our family dog. My sister-in-law, who is a professional nurse and amateur hair cutter, regularly gives her husband (a nice man with a small head) buzz cuts, and she volunteered to use her clippers (with the #2 attachment) on me. The result was nothing short of a hair disaster. I looked like I had just been paroled from San Quentin—which reminds me: in Modesto, that was the summer of wife-murderer Scott Peterson, and he was sporting the same jailhouse hairdo. In fact, while I had the buzz cut, one of my college students, big Earl Crawford, asked, "Hey Doc, anybody over there in Modesto ever tell you that you kinda look like that Scott Peterson dude?" I responded that no one had ever said that, but once my wife's aunt and uncle had said I looked like actor Dean Cain, who, coincidentally, was at that time playing Scott Peterson in a TV movie.

neighborhood Hair Masters, formerly Haircuts 2000, sitting in a barber chair and looking in the mirror, when I became completely mesmerized by my own forehead. This fascination must have gone on for more than a few minutes because the "stylist" stopped cutting and asked, "What's wrong? Is there something you don't like?"

"Oh, no," I said. "I was just looking at my forehead. Look how big it is! There's room for me to have another face up there."

The stylist didn't know what to say. On one hand, she was clearly relieved that I was not unhappy with her work, but she did not know what to do with a "client" making an offbeat and self-deprecating joke. I shut up after this exchange and then gave her a $1 tip when she was done. I walked out of the "salon" feeling as I usually do after a haircut: dubious about the cut and uncomfortable with the experience. I do not like going to the haircutting places, but where is a 40-year-old, bigheaded, thick-haired white man supposed to go? There aren't many traditional barbershops left, and I don't think I would come home with a cut that would be acceptable to my wife.

Speaking of my wife, she did talk me into trying (twice) the real salon where she gets her hair done, but I might as well get my hair done at a haunted house. The stylists there tend to be outrageously gay men or sexy women, who, prior to cutting your hair, willingly massage your scalp while they shampoo your hair.

It's a no-win situation.

Ron the Barber

When we moved to Carbondale, Illinois in August of 1989, Paula and I began a life of adjustments—to each other, to raging humidity, to a large university in a small town, to a horizon without mountains. But for me the hardest adjustment was finding a decent place to get my hair cut. A few weeks after we arrived in Carbondale, I realized that it was time for me to get a haircut. I looked up "Barbers" in the Yellow Pages and found a shop located in the Mur-dale Shopping Center.[32] I don't remember exactly, but I must have gone in on a Saturday because the shop was quite busy. The shop had five or six chairs, which were all full, and

---

[32] "Mur-dale" is the name given to an area on the west side of Carbondale and the east side of the next town over, Murphysboro; hence, Mur-dale. Clever.

several men and boys were sitting in the waiting area. The barbers working there were mostly older guys, and they wore identical uniforms. When I got in the chair, I had little confidence that the man cutting my hair understood what I asked him to do. The haircut looked okay when the barber finished, but he hadn't thinned out my thick hair at all, nor had he taken off enough from the top or the sides. In a week or two, I looked like one of the Beatles (and not the cute one).

For my next haircut, we decided that I should try going to a salon recommended by one of our new acquaintances. This salon was located on a piece of property in downtown Carbondale, almost adjacent to the university, that we later learned was owned, or co-owned, by a senior member of the SIU English faculty. The salon was in the basement of the main building (which was very old) on this property. The building also housed a Chinese restaurant/bar that was popular with many of the heavy drinkers and vegetarians in our English department. I suppose it would have been better if the first hair salon I ever visited were a cleaner, more well lighted place. The person in the salon who cut my hair was certainly not an old man. She was young and blonde, and she wore a tight, purple mini-skirt. When this person cut my hair, she innocently but repeatedly leaned and rubbed against my body. She was not that tall, and apparently she had trouble reaching the top of my massive head. As a husband of only a few months, I couldn't help but feel that I was behaving inappropriately just by sitting in the chair. Over the next four years (three in Carbondale, one in Springfield, Missouri) I never went to the same salon more than twice.

Admittedly, the need for a haircut may not seem like legitimate cause for a psychological, and even existential (if you don't recognize yourself), crisis. I also admit that I should have been able to let the little blonde girl do her job without it bothering me, and I should have been able to tell the old man at the barbershop exactly how I wanted my hair cut. However, I had never had my hair cut by anyone who was shorter or prettier than I am, and I had never really needed to give a barber much instruction. How is this possible? Well, when I got married at the age of twenty three, my hair had been cut by exactly three people: my dad,[33] Ron (owner of Ron's Barbershop), and Vern (a man who worked for Ron and later opened his own barbershop, called Vern's Barbershop).

Ron's Barbershop featured three chairs that were staffed by Ron, Vern, and another guy whose name I do not remember, but I'll call him Larry. I don't recall Larry ever cutting my hair, but I do remember that we decided his work was unacceptable. Maybe he

---

[33] Like most of the dads in my neighborhood, my dad went through a period in which he thought he could cut our hair just as easily as some barber—and save money in the process. So he had my mom buy some clippers. Amazingly, with no training at all, dad soon perfected "the Butch"—which is what we called the buzz cut in the old days. My lasting dislike of the buzz cut is at least partly due to dad's "butchery" of my hair. Plus, the butch was a symbol of punishment for naughty boys. It signified that the boy's parents wished they had the money to send him to reform school. Dad's barbering lasted about 2 or 3 cuts before we sought professional help. The professional we found was Ron.

botched my brother's hair and that was enough. So when we blackballed Larry we were forced to tell him we would wait for Ron or Vern, even if Larry was free and there were other guys waiting in line for Ron and Vern. I don't know what happened to Larry, but he didn't stay at Ron's Barbershop for very long. Vern, on the other hand, worked at Ron's for several years before opening his own shop. While my dad liked Vern's work and even went to him after he left Ron, my brother and I were never Vern fans. We felt that Vern's trademark style, the uneven Hitler-youth haircut, was not a cool look for the 1970s.[34]

Actually, our preference for Ron was probably all about being cool. Even though we knew virtually nothing about him, Ron was one of the coolest adults we had ever encountered. For one thing, he had long hair—neatly coifed, parted in the middle, feathered back, early-seventies rock star hair. Granted this was the hippie era, but most of the grown men in Modesto, including my dad and most of Ron's customers, were still combing their hair American Graffiti-style—with plenty of Brilcream.[35] I realize now that what made Ron interesting then and memorable still was that he

---

[34] It's laughable now that we were such discerning and discriminating customers, considering that at the time approximately 90% of all lower-middle class white boys had their hair cut like Moe Howard (sometimes called the "Pete Rose"). The other 10% were being punished with the Butch.
[35] I don't want to denigrate the early-sixties greased back look. It was plenty cool in its day. And because Modesto *was* the home of George Lucas and American Graffiti, it probably stayed cool longer than in other places. My parents knew people who knew people who inspired some of the characters in Lucas's movie. Actually, my dad could have been the mysterious hot rodder from out of town.

maintained an unconventional persona in the most conventional and traditional environment. He catered to his conventional clientele, giving them the cuts they wanted while using only the electric clippers. He sold them the kinds of hair products they wanted and kept the shop in the manner one would expect in a traditional barbershop.

Ron's Barbershop was located in a rather non-descript shopping center (today, we would classify it as a strip mall). The main store in the shopping center was called (and still is today) Sam's Food City. My mother claimed to have once seen a butcher in Sam's scratch his head with his hand and then go back to working with some ground beef without washing, so we never shopped there. Sam's took up most of the building space and faced the street (Carver Road). Next to Sam's (on the right, looking from the street) was a liquor store. The liquor store was located on the corner of the building, and to get to Ron's we had to go around the corner of the building, where there was a strip of three or four shops. These shops were not visible from Carver Road, but each had a sign hanging from the front of the building. Ron's shop was next to a beauty salon whose interior seemed as mysterious to me as deepest darkest Africa. Ron always kept a sign indicating his current prices for various cuts and ages hanging in the front window of his shop. He also had a sign that read "We trim long hair" in all capital letters, with L-O-N-G printed at least 4 times as tall as the other letters.

The three barber chairs were lined down the left wall of the small, narrow shop. There was a mirror behind each chair and a mirror across from each chair on the opposite wall. There was also a small, I assume, storage room in the back (or far end) where Ron swept all the cut hair that fell on the shop floor. On the back wall next to the door to the storage room there hung an official-looking poster that appeared to have been printed by some government agency. This poster had a heading in bold letters that read "In Case of Nuclear Attack," and below the heading was a list of instructions for the average citizen to follow if such an emergency occurred. All of the instructions seemed logical and practical until the last one. The last instruction said something like "Bend over, put your head between your knees, and kiss your ass goodbye."

I also remember a wooden plaque between two of the mirrors on the wall opposite the barber chairs that offered this proverb: "Better to remain silent and be thought a fool than to open your mouth and remove all doubt." I know there were other funny signs featuring high-quality sophomoric humor, but I have forgotten them after all these years. What I do remember is that as I got older the jokes I heard told in the barbershop got progressively cruder.

* * *

Ron cut my hair for the next-to-last-time about a week before I got married. I don't think he had any idea that I was getting my hair cut for such a special occasion. And I really don't know if he noticed that one of his regulars had stopped coming in after I moved away. My hair looks pretty good in our wedding photographs—if the viewer of the pictures keeps in mind that it was the late eighties. The hair is parted basically in the middle of my big head. I have bangs that are separated on my forehead. The sides are combed back a bit, and there is just the slightest hint of a mullet in the back.[36] As I said before, I was twenty-three when I got married, and I stuck with this same hairstyle (despite my inability to find a suitable hair cutter anywhere in the southern Midwest) until I was twenty-seven, almost twenty-eight, on the verge of receiving my PhD. We were living in Springfield, Missouri by that time, and we were preparing to go back to Carbondale for the Summer Term commencement at SIU. I woke up one day and decided that I should comb my hair like a grown man. So we went to some shopping mall salon and I got it cut so that I could part it on the side and keep the front off my forehead. Thirteen years later, as my forehead grows larger, I'm re-considering my hairstyle again. For now I'm just letting it grow a little long—for that eccentric

---

[36] When did this style start being called a mullet? I don't remember ever hearing the word "mullet" in the eighties. Is mullet a hockey term?

professor/writer look. I'm afraid, though, I look more like Billy Graham or Oral Roberts.

I think it was Jerry Seinfeld who did a bit about how men seem to reach a certain age where they decide to stop changing the style of the clothes, their hair, their shoes, their everything—forever. You can look at a man of a certain age and tell when he stopped changing (or trying): plaid shirt, powder-blue sans-a-belt pants = late 1970s. When I went back to Ron for the last time in late 1993 (a few months after the aforementioned style change), I realized Ron had become one of these guys Seinfeld was talking about. Not only was the shop exactly the same as it was when I was six years old, but so was Ron. He had a little more stomach and some gray hair, but he still sported the same '70s hair and the clothes to match. I guess I hadn't noticed as I was growing up that he wasn't changing. But now (in 1993) it was painfully obvious.

When I entered the shop there was an instant recognition. It wasn't a "Don't I know you?" kind of recognition, though. It was more like, "Hey, you haven't been in the shop for a while." I explained that I had been out of the state for four years, had gotten married, earned a PhD, and fathered a soon-to-be-born child. Then he cut my hair. And I have to say it was an excellent cut. However, when I paid for the haircut and I walked out of the shop, I knew I wouldn't be back. Returning to California after four years had produced some strange feelings about a lot of things, but going back into Ron's Barbershop was just too frightening. Maybe you can go home again, but you can't go home to your barber.

Houndini

Paula and I moved out of Evergreen Terrace for a beagle.[37] Although many residents of Evergreen Terrace defied the rules by having tropical fish, hamsters, and even a kitty or two, the housing complex enforced a zero-tolerance no-pet policy. And for some reason, we thought life would be richer and more meaningful if we had a dog.[38] So at the end of our first academic year in Carbondale, we found a fairly nice place to live in

---

[37] Paula insists that I include a note here indicating that there were other reasons for us to move out of Evergreen Terrace, such as the Chinese people who lived below us and boiled the most pungent fish I have ever smelled. It occurs to me that I have called my own veracity into question. I apologize.

[38] Any reader who has taken Introduction to Psychology is now surmising that the dog was probably a substitute child and merely a response to our instinctual need to start a family.

the country, just south of town. A family with young children had recently built a new house on the southeast corner of a twenty-acre soybean field.[39] Behind the house, they built a rental property, a duplex. The back doors of each unit in the duplex faced south and opened out onto two small, identical decks. The front doors, though, were on opposite sides of the building. For one unit, the front door faced east and opened into the main house's backyard. The other unit, which we rented, faced west, and the small front porch looked out to the soybean field and beyond that a wooded area.

To get to our new home we had to travel about ½ mile down a gravel road, along which there were other small farms, horse properties, and such. It was a great place to bring up a hound, though a beagle was not our first choice. We named her Olivia, Livy for short, and we bought her from an old farmer who lived on an old farm and raised beagles for hunting purposes. Livy was a delightful pup. To begin with, beagle pups are ridiculously cute. They are energetic and good-natured, without being annoying or spastic.[40] Their sweet disposition belies the fact that they are pack animals (that is, they run in packs; they don't carry packs like mules or donkeys) and scent hounds with little need for a lot of human

---

[39] I think the land had been inherited from the wife's parents.
[40] Our friends, Doug and Anna Emanus, got a black cocker spaniel named Otto (after the bus driver on "The Simpsons") at about the same time we got Livy. Otto was hyperactive, unpredictable, and just plain stupid. However, this last characteristic may not be a bad one in the long run.

attention. In short, beagles are smart and instinctive animals—often too smart and too instinctive for their own good.

*　*　*

Livy grew up, by virtue of the rural location of our duplex, largely unencumbered by the restrictions placed on a city dog, especially a California dog. Most dogs in California live their lives in fenced backyards, waiting for those precious moments when their owners take them out into the great wide world.[41] Dogs in the Midwest in contrast, live in a world without privacy fences, and therefore must have a broader worldview and greater opportunity to go abroad. But a country hound, like Livy, is the Huckleberry Finn (Huckleberry Hound, if you prefer) of the dog world. Sure, we tried to keep her tethered to a rope or chain in the yard around our side of the duplex, and Paula even took her to dog obedience training. It soon became apparent, though, that Livy would live by the rules of nature, and our efforts to contain her (which would last the next ten years) were mostly futile and frustrating.

We learned first that keeping her tied up as a means to prevent her from running away and getting lost was completely

---

[41] Our current dog Sally, a terrier-corgi mix, is a bizarre exception to this rule. She has no desire to see the world or even her own backyard. Sally has only one thing for which to live: chasing her ball down the hallway. Otherwise she's content to curl up on the sofa or in her kennel.

unnecessary. Although over the years Livy's disappearing acts would become increasingly troublesome and problematic (more on that later), she was biologically incapable of getting lost. No matter how far she roamed, her nose would always lead her home, unless of course her nose had first led her into serious trouble. When Livy picked up a scent, her tail picked up and straightened, the hair along her back stood up, and her nose dropped to the ground. And she started howling, like someone was beating her to death. Her pursuit of the scent could lead her anywhere, including places she was not welcome. So we did have some reason to try to keep her close to home. But she was relentless, and we often relented—which in turn led to enormous veterinary bills.[42]

    We knew that the next-door neighbors didn't like Livy or the other dogs in the area because they felt the dogs bothered their horses. But I have no proof that the neighbors were responsible for shooting Livy. She came home one night in especially bad shape (she would often come home in a pretty raggedy condition), and when we took a look at her it looked like her hindquarter had been sprayed with pea gravel. So we took her to the vet, who said he was pretty sure she had been peppered with a little shogun shot. Then there was the time she came home with a swollen muzzle, apparently from a bite or sting. Ironically, the worst scrape Livy

---

[42] I hope we are not the only people to use student loan money for a dog's doctor bills.

ever suffered happened when she was walking with me. As I said before, our duplex was located ½ mile down a gravel road, and the gravel road continued past the place we lived for another ½ mile before it reached a dead end in the woods. We often took the dog for walks down to the end of the road and back. Most of the time I kept her on a retractable lead, but one day when I let her run freely we encountered a big, mean dog. To be fair, the dog was on his own property, a good seventy-five feet from where I stood in the road. The dog announced his menacing presence with several deep barks and some growling. Before I could catch her, Livy ran toward the dog and onto its property. She stopped about ten feet short of the big dog, and for a moment it looked like it might be a harmless standoff. The other dog, who had a history of aggressive behavior, appeared to be content with simply intimidating my little dog. Livy, on her side, didn't want a fight, but I knew she wouldn't be able to keep her big mouth shut for long.

    I did not want to start a fracas by yelling at the dogs, so I called to Livy softly and hurried toward her. But I never really had a chance. She erupted in her blood-curdling yet harmless howl, and the other dog pounced on her like she was a squeaky chew toy. His jaws wrapped around her neck, and he picked her up and shook her. By this time, I was yelling and throwing rocks at the dog, and he eventually dropped Livy and ran off. Livy appeared to be hurt but not seriously injured. When I got her home, I inspected her puncture wounds. They looked superficial to me and she wasn't bleeding at all, so I figured we had dodged a bullet. For the next few days, Livy slowed down a bit, but she seemed fine otherwise. Then one day I noticed that the left side of the dog's head was enlarged. Livy's hound dog jowls had begun to swell, and by the time I got her in to the veterinarian her head has become grossly misshapen. As Livy's luck would have it, the big dog's bite had punctured her salivary gland, which allowed fluid to leak into the tissue under the skin of her face—instead of draining normally.

The vet took immediate action. He cut holes in the top and the bottom of Livy's jowl and inserted a rubber tube, or shunt, that ran from the top hole through her cheek and out the bottom. He then gave me a medicine bottle that contained a foul-smelling iodine-based liquid. Twice a day I had to squirt this medicine, using an eyedropper, into the top hole of the dog's jowl. The shunt would allow fluid to drain until the wound healed. The medicine, which was not easy to administer because I had to get the end of the dropper in between the tube and her flesh, simply prevented infection. The hardest job, though, was keeping Livy out of further trouble until she could recover from the injury.[43]

---

[43] The reader may have noticed that Paula was not mentioned at all during the salivary gland episode. She, as fate would have it, was out of town. She went to Pensacola, Florida with our friend Anna, who had to go there to be in a wedding. Paula went along to help look after Anna's baby boy, Nicholas. So for a week it was just me, the dog, and the medicine dropper.

Livy endured other, more minor, incidents in her two years out on Rural Route 3. She would regularly come home from her jaunts fatigued to the point of utter exhaustion—the very epitome of dog-tired. On many of these jaunts she was accompanied by her good friend, the chocolate lab. The chocolate lab, whose name we never knew, lived down the lane, and he exuded the same sweet disposition and boundless energy that Livy had. I do not remember how the two dogs met. Although we knew where he lived, we did not know the lab's owners, and, as I said, we didn't even know the dog's name. But at some point the dogs developed their own daily hunting routine. For quite a while, the chocolate lab showed up on the lawn outside our duplex every morning. He would wait with that look of happy-dog expectation on his face until we let Livy out of the house. When we let Livy out, they briefly exchanged pleasantries, and then they were off. Often we would not see them again until after nightfall. But like a gentleman, the lab always brought Livy home before going home himself. I wish we still had a picture of the two dogs together. They made quite a hunting team: the scent hound and the sight retriever. They were the doggy odd couple.[44]

To tell an interesting/bizarre/funny story about Livy and the chocolate lab I have to make sure the reader knows a little bit about deer hunting in Illinois. First, white tail deer are everywhere in the

---

[44] I wonder if Neil Simon would go for a canine version of The Odd Couple.

state, especially in southern Illinois. So for many hunters a deer-hunting trip consists of a walk out into the backyard. Because the deer are in such close proximity to people and buildings, deer hunters in Illinois are not allowed to use deer rifles. A rifle bullet could end up in someone's living room. Instead, a hunter is required to use a shotgun loaded with a deer slug. "Deer season" takes place during designated weekends when everybody and his dense brother-in-law walks out into the woods, hides in a deer stand, and shoots at everything with a white tail.

Our place on the edge of the soybean field was often a deer superhighway. There were many mornings and evenings when we saw dozens of deer moving across the field from one thicket to another. Our landlord, like most of the men in the neighborhood, was an avid hunter, and as deer season approached he went out across the soybean field and into the woods to prepare his deer stand. Then on the first day of the season we saw him and his friends walk out from the house with their guns. A few minutes after they disappeared in the woods, we heard the firing of the shotguns. The landlord then came back to the house, got into his old Chevy 4X4 truck, and drove it around the edge of the field and into the woods. We soon realized that the deer had been loaded into the pickup bed and brought back to the edge of the field. When they got close to the yard, they stopped the truck and field-dressed the deer right there, burying much of the innards somewhere out in the field.

We held Livy against her will in the house for the duration of the deer season weekend. We knew that if Livy were out there in the woods with the deer and the hunters, she would be shot the instant she got a scent in her nose and started her beagle bellowing. As soon as the hunters finished their pursuit of Bambi, though, Livy and the chocolate lab were back on the trail doing their kind of hunting. The first day they were able to get out and roam again Livy and the lab were gone from sunrise to sunset. When she returned, I heard Livy on our wooden front porch and let her in the house. She looked like a kid who had spent the day at an amusement park, riding thrill rides and eating every possible kind of junk food. I noticed her eyes were glossed over and her stomach was bloated as she walked in the short entryway of the duplex. When Livy stepped off the linoleum of the entry way and onto the carpet of our small family room, she stopped and made an odd gulping sound. Her stomach convulsed, her mouth opened, and out plopped an organ! The whole hurling process took maybe five seconds, but I'm sure it took longer for me to realize what had just happened.

Let me make this perfectly clear: the dog regurgitated (maybe that's the wrong word) a complete internal deer organ. I ascertained that it wasn't one of Livy's organs because she felt much better after expelling it. This organ was absolutely whole, with no visible signs of damage, other than the fact that it had been extracted from the animal that owned it. I'm no anatomy expert, so I never knew for sure what organ it was. It was a dark red, almost purple, color, and it was more oblong than round. The organ was probably five or six inches long and perhaps four inches thick. And even though I saw Livy hurl the organ on the carpet, to this day I can't understand how she could swallow that thing, which was bigger than her mouth and her gullet, get it down in her gut, and then send it back out without disturbing its structural integrity.

Knowing Livy, though, I can imagine how she came to possess the organ in her stomach. So if the reader can forgive my conjecture, I'll briefly relate the events of Livy's organ adventure. Livy and the chocolate lab had a field day (pardon the pun) the day after deer season, with fresh scents in the air everywhere and new trails beaten down all over the woods. Eventually, Livy picked up a beautifully rancid smell practically in her own backyard. A few feet of dirt was no match for her nose. Livy led the lab to the gut burial ground, and the digging was easy for the two of them in the freshly turned soil. Within seconds they hit the mother lode. They dragged the parts out of the hole, and rubbed their noses in everything. At some point, the lab probably stopped playing and called to Livy: "Check this out," at which point he showed Livy how he could swallow a disgusting deer part.

"You're sick," Livy said in response.

"Betcha can't do it."

"Maybe I don't wanna do it."

"You're just scared."

"No, I'm not."

"Then have an organ."

"Okay, but mine's gonna be bigger than the one you swallowed." And the rest is gastrointestinal history. Livy got the organ down like a garter snake eating a rat, and she answered the lab's dare. Of course, Livy was then sick as a dog, but she wasn't going to let the lab see her throw up. Since it was already getting dark, she suggested they go home for some real dinner. The lab dropped her off at our yard and went home. Livy struggled up the two steps of the front porch and managed a single scratch at the door. Safely out of her friend's view, Livy immediately hocked up that which did not belong in her stomach on the brown carpet.

Surprisingly, there were no lingering effects requiring payment to the veterinarian because of this particular escapade. One time, not long before we left Carbondale for Springfield, Missouri, the dog and I had a narrow escape from what I thought was certain disaster. I took her for a walk down our gravel road, the same one where she suffered her punctured gland, this time on the retractable lead. We walked to the end of the road, and on the way back, as we passed through a low section of the road, I saw a skunk just thirty feet away. The skunk was walking in the same direction we were through an open bit of meadow in the broad daylight. Livy couldn't see the skunk because the embankment on either side of the road was about chest high. But I wasn't concerned about Livy seeing the skunk. I was worried about her nose. One sniff of that skunk, and Livy would start bellowing—which just might disturb our striped friend.

I was in a bit of a quandary. If I tried to hustle Livy away, I could rile her up, or I might agitate the skunk myself. But continuing along as we were gave Livy more time to smell. So without saying anything to Livy, I just starting walking faster—all the while watching the skunk for any sign of disturbance. Remarkably, the skunk soon turned and sidled into the woods on the other side of the clearing. At that point, I picked up Livy's pace to a near-sprint for about fifty yards. And we escaped, for once.

* * *

The more I think about Livy and her adventures I realize on the one hand how much time and energy she required in the middle of a busy and eventful time, but still it's hard to imagine going through those experiences without the dog right there. There is a picture of the dog and me in the spare bedroom of the little house we rented in Springfield, Missouri. I am sitting, reclining really, in our old wooden desk chair in front of the computer. I am working on my dissertation. Note cards are spread all around the desk, along with a few books. Behind me is a window that looks out into the front yard. Normally, I would have the keyboard in my lap and my feet up on the desk, but in the picture there is Livy with her body facing the window and her head turned back toward the camera. I know the reader doesn't care, but my dissertation was about contemporary American women writers who had created female characters in search of a typically male freedom. These female characters flee conventional roles, and try to live a life of adventure and escape. Eventually, though, living on the road and being different takes a toll. The women, unlike most of their male counterparts, try to find an elusive balance between freedom and security. I think that kind of existence was what Livydog embodied.[45] She wanted to roam free, but she needed a home base where she could lick her wounds, eat some Ol' Roy and table scraps, and drink clean water. But, alas, living an unconventional life is as hard for a dog as it is for a woman.

When we moved to Springfield, we discovered that Livy had the ability to extricate herself from any backyard, if she so desired. Livy had never been in a backyard, per se, and she did not appreciate having new restrictions on her ability to move. It was a nice backyard, bigger than many, with a chain link fence all around it. The fence looked secure enough for an ordinary dog, but after Livy escaped a few times, we often resorted to putting a chain on her. The funny thing about her escapes (and this would be true at

---

[45] Admittedly, this theory sounds preposterous, even to me.

later residences as well) was that I couldn't always tell how or where she got out.

In an effort to compensate for the loss of her freedom to roam, I took Livy for regular long walks. Fortunately, the city of Springfield had built a large sports complex adjacent to our neighborhood.[46] The sports complex contained several softball and baseball diamonds, as well as soccer fields. The area was nicely landscaped, and there was a concrete path that meandered around the whole complex. Virtually every afternoon or evening, Livy and I walked from our house on N. Elmwood, through our neighborhood, to the park, and around the loop. These walks served several purposes: Livy expended some of her energy; I enjoyed watching the little leaguers play ball; I used the time to work through problems with the dissertation; and, most importantly, the walks enabled me to work out the frustration of an endless stream of rejections from potential employers.

One hot, sticky evening Livy and I went out for a walk, and as we began to circle around the park the clouds in the sky began to organize themselves into giant thunderheads. We kept walking as the wind picked up. The ballplayers, coaches, and fans took notice of the sudden changes in weather as the first sprinkles hit the

---

[46] Springfield is an unusual city in that the south side is the desirable area of town. Newer, upscale stores and restaurants are in the south part of town, as are the nicer neighborhoods. Paula and I lived on the north side, which tends to be poorer and more industrial.

ground. Livy and I picked up our pace when the thunder and lightning began, but we stopped in our tracks when the tornado warning sirens started blaring.[47] In an instant the park and its visitors were in an uproar. Parents grabbed their kids as players ran off the fields. Coaches grabbed their equipment, and everyone ran for their cars in the parking lot. But no one made it to the lot before the clouds burst and the rain just dumped buckets on everyone. Meanwhile, Livy and I had to think of plan B. We were close to ½ mile from home and getting there on foot in the storm would be no fun at all (and perhaps dangerously stupid). We cut across the grass and headed toward the east end of the parking lot (on the south side of the park) where there was a building that housed public bathrooms. By the time we reached the bathroom, all the players, fans, and coaches had cleared out and retreated to the relative safety of their homes. Luckily, the bathroom was lighted, ventilated, and clean.

---

[47] I would just like to point out again that it makes no sense to live in the lower Midwest, especially if you don't have a storm cellar. Whenever we told a local person (either in Illinois or Missouri) that we were from California, the typical response went something like this: "How can you live out there with all them earthquakes?" I would answer, "How can you live here knowing that a mobile home might land in your yard at any time?" All of us are familiar with the tests of the Emergency Broadcast System on radio and TV, but neither Paula nor I had ever heard an actual warning until we moved to the Midwest. In one year in Springfield, we found ourselves huddled in the bathroom (with Livy, the computer floppy disks that contained my dissertation, and our wedding picture album) of our cellar-less house four or five times, waiting for the tornado warning to pass.

Livy was a bit antsy as I resigned myself to waiting out the storm in the men's room. I stood by the door and held it open an inch or two to monitor the rain. After a few minutes we heard a vehicle coming close, and then we saw headlights shining through the crack in the door. I pushed the door open a little farther, and there was Paula in our trusty Dodge Colt. Because there was a driveway of sorts at the corner of the parking lot (so service vehicles could drive on to the park grounds), she was able to drive to within ten or fifteen feet of the bathroom door. Livy and I made a break for the Colt. I hopped in the passenger seat and Livy jumped in my lap. Paula said she saw the storm brewing at home, but she figured we would be okay. Then she heard the warning siren go off, and she sprang into action. Paula drove the Colt to the park and began looking for us. The back part of the park borders a local airport, so she couldn't drive all the way around the park. But she could tell we were no longer on the path. Paula was driving through the parking lot when she spied the sliver of light emitting from the slightly open bathroom door. She could barely see through the windshield of the Colt, but she knew the bathroom was the only place we could be.[48]

By the time we got home, the above ground drainage ditches that lined the streets of our neighborhood were running full. We parked in our driveway, behind our other car (a 1990 Ford Tempo), which was under the carport, and the three of us ducked into the

---

[48] Have I mentioned that I married a hell of a gal, and I'm lucky she married me.

house as quickly as we could. In thirty minutes the rain was gone, and in an hour or two the drainage ditches had finished their work—just another day in Springfield, Missouri.

* * *

Livy was a traveler, not just a roamer. When we made trips to California at Christmas and during summer breaks, Livy preferred to ride in the front seat of our Tempo, propped up on several pillows so that she could see out the window while lying down.[49] And when we came home for good (and bad) in the summer of 1993, she rode shotgun with me in the Ryder truck for the entire trip. Unfortunately for Livy, life in California was no improvement over Missouri. We moved into a small, old duplex with a miniscule backyard, and we prepared to welcome our first child in the winter of 1994.[50] In less than a year, we were able to rent a small but delightful house on the

---

[49] Once, during a Christmas break trip, we stopped at a rest stop in the Flagstaff, Arizona, area, and the snow was deeper than any Livy had ever seen in Illinois. She hopped out of the car to take a leak. But when she hit that snow, she tried to figure out a way to walk without any of her four paws actually touching the snow. The back two went up, then the front. Then she tried to balance one foot. I don't remember if she ever got comfortable enough to pee.

[50] Livy didn't roam much in our months at the duplex, largely because our new vet in Turlock discovered that she had kidney stones and needed surgery. I have no idea how we paid that bill. It was such a peculiar ailment that the vet put them on display in his waiting room. I never asked the vet if a swallowed deer organ could have caused the stones. Livy also developed a skin allergy to something in her new environment. We applied an ointment to her skin, and she then rubbed her side on our sofa, which left a greasy stain that never came out.

wrong side of Turlock. The house was situated on a narrow but incredibly deep lot. When we walked out the back door, there was a small yard/patio area that was about 20' X 20'. It was bordered on the left by the property line/fence, on the right by the small, detached garage, and on the far side by a wire fence that had a gate that opened into the backyard proper. This main backyard was big enough for a large lawn, a vegetable garden, and an old shed, and it should have provided Livy with more than enough room to keep her happy. Instead, she entered her full-blown Houndini stage.

The house was located in a very old neighborhood, and many of the yards had what one might call makeshift fences. The mish mash of wire and picket fences around our yard was no match for a dog of Livy's talents. She began to get out regularly, and I tried to shore up each place in the fence where she found a weakness. But it was no use because the soil in Turlock, especially on the Westside, is quite sandy. No matter how much I built up the fence, there was always another place along the fence line where she could easily dig a tunnel deep enough for her to escape.[51] Then we tried leaving her in the house while we were gone, so at least we wouldn't have to go look for her when we returned. We put her in the laundry room/service porch. There was no door into the area, and we had to block off the doorway as best we could because we didn't want her

---

[51] The back fence was especially vulnerable because that was the garden area and there was no lawn along the fence to firm up the soil.

to have free reign in the house. We bought one of those baby gates that can be put across doorways to keep kids and pets where one wants them. We put the dog in the room. We put up the gate. When we came home, the dog was at the front door to greet us. An investigation of the premises revealed that the gate was exactly where we left it. This failure to contain the dog in the utility room led to repeated efforts to reinforce and expand the gate. And every time we came home, the dog had escaped her confinement. I wish I could have put up a surveillance camera to record how she did it—just to see the master in action.

Sometimes when Livy got out of the yard, we would find her on the neighbor's side of the fence. Other escapes were more successful, though, and I often found myself combing the neighborhood, searching for the dog. One warm night, when Emily, our reluctant sleeper, was about eighteen months old, she couldn't fall asleep because our next-door neighbor was blaring mariachi music about a foot from Emily's bedroom window. It was late and the neighbor was drunk, and I went outside to yell at him.[52] He was feeling macho and confrontational, and I was trying to think of any Spanish cuss words I could holler at him. Just as the argument was about to get interesting (I wasn't too worried because he wasn't

---

[52] This particular neighbor was the patriarch of a multi-generational Mexican family. He was apparently a dairy worker, judging from his boots. He typically came home from work around two or three in the afternoon with a twelve pack of Bud Light. He drank the beer until he got drowsy, and then he slept for a few hours on the lawn.

armed, and he wasn't walking too well), Paula discovered that, of course, the dog was missing. So I dropped the argument and decided to address two problems at once. I put Emily in her car seat and buckled her in the backseat of the Tempo. Then we went out looking for the hound. I hoped that Emily would fall asleep or at least get drowsy as I patrolled the neighborhood.

    I rolled down the windows of the car, and Emily and I began calling out for Livy. We didn't yell too loudly because it was getting late, and we did not want to disturb the neighborhood. We criss-crossed the streets around our house without any luck. It wasn't like I was worried that Livy couldn't find her way home. I knew she wasn't lost. But she could easily get hit by a car or mauled by one of the neighborhood's many pit bulls. After a while, Emily and I came back around to our street, Park Street, and we drove past our house, moving east toward Broadway Avenue. At the corner of Park and Broadway there is a park (imagine that), and we turned left (north) onto Broadway and drove by the west side of the park. As we moved up Broadway, I thought I heard a noise, so I slowed to almost a stop and turned the radio all the way off. I glanced, by chance, in my driver's side mirror and saw what had made the clickety-clackety noise that I had heard. It was Livy, running right down the middle of Broadway, on the yellow line. When she neared the car, I simply opened my driver's door, and with no hesitation she hopped into the car, across my lap, and into the passenger seat. She sat up in the seat, panting but otherwise nonplussed, as if to say, "Take me home now, young man." Emily, still awake in the car seat behind me, was pleased our doggie had found us.

* * *

Our second daughter, Abigail, was born in the winter of 1996, and a few months later we were able to buy a house in Modesto.[53] This last move marked the beginning of the end for Livy's stay with the Schmidt family. Livy got off to a rough start her first day in her new backyard. Our house has a small in-ground swimming pool, and on that first day it had a solar blanket covering it. Livy had no previous experience with either a swimming pool or a solar blanket, so she promptly walked out on to the blanket. The world suddenly became very unstable for her, and she might have drowned under the blanket. But I saw the whole incident and fished her out without any further trouble.

It took Livy a few months to get comfortable enough with her new surroundings for her to start up with her old tricks. First, she found every weak board in the fence. Once I shored up the fence, she resorted to the old standby: digging out. I filled in the

---

[53] Ten years later, we still live in the same house. Thanks to a super-heated real estate market in California (which has finally started to cool down), our house is no longer a $105, 000 starter home. It's a $350, 000 starter home.

holes, and she dug out again practically before the shovel was put away in the garage. So then I began putting bricks in the holes before I filled in the dirt. Thus began the ugly final phase of my relationship with Livydog. With two little girls, a house, and a full-time (finally) teaching position, I didn't have the time or the will to worry about a dog that wouldn't stay in the yard. She made me so mad. Now that the yard actually belonged to us, I did not want Livy constantly destroying it. So I took a perfectly reasonable approach to dealing with her: I began chasing her around the yard with the shovel and yelling, "I'm gonna kill you if you dig one more hole!" Looking back, I understand that this approach was not particularly effective, nor was it healthy for the kids. They used to stand at the sliding patio door and holler, "Mom, come here. Dad is going to kill the dog with the shovel!" For the record, I never really hurt the dog, and I think Livy enjoyed the exercise.

    Livy was like an old egg-sucking dog; I couldn't break her habit. I even gave up going out and looking for her. She had a dog license, and her tag had our telephone and address on it. When she got out, we just waited for her to come home or for someone in the neighborhood to call. Of course, all the neighbors needed to do was leave Livy alone (she couldn't get lost), or shoo her away if she was being a nuisance. I realize that doesn't sound like responsible dog ownership, but walk a mile in my shoes (looking for a beagle).

One night, or morning rather, around 3:00 a.m., I was awakened by a noise at the front door. I got up to investigate, and as I came down the hall to the door I heard it again. It was a combination scratch-bump sort of sound. At that time, we had a security-screen door on the outside of the front door, so I opened the front door without fear of dire consequences. When I opened the door, I saw that it was Livy on the other side of the screen. I thought, "No freakin' way." I began to feel like Barney Fife on that episode of the *Andy Griffith Show* where the boys can't keep Ernest T. Bass in his jail cell. At one point, when Barney is about to explode in anger, Ernest T. just smiles and says, "Irritatin', ain't it?" I like to think Livy was having as much fun with me as Ernest T. did with Barney and Andy. Her appearance at the front door was the crime that forced me to lay down the law, once and for all.

The next morning, when I looked for her escape point, I discovered that she had, amazingly, gone out under the back fence, which meant she had traveled a good distance just to get back to our front door. Our neighbor behind us (Ron) lives in the center lot of a cul-de-sac (we called it a "court" in the old days). And when Livy went into Ron's backyard, she had to find a way through either one of his side yard gates. Then she would find herself in the cul-de-sac. When she moved to the mouth of the court, she could go either left or right in order to go all the way around the block to our house. But either way she went, she faced two "intersections" where she had to choose the correct direction to take. Depending on whether she went left or right from the cul-de-sac, the trip around the loop to our house was a distance of ¼ mile or ½ mile. For Livy, such a jaunt was a piece of cake. I'm sure she didn't break out of our yard only to make the trip around the block back to our house. Certainly, she found the empty field not far from the next street over from us. She may have even gone to the park adjacent to our neighborhood elementary school. Livy had been there many times on the leash.

By the time I lost all patience with Livy it must have been 1999. And even though the dog was approaching ten years of age, she showed no signs of slowing down. So we did the unthinkable. No, I didn't hit her with the shovel; I just convinced Paula that it was time to give her away. Paula placed a classified advertisement in the *Modesto Bee*, and the first people who came to take a look at Livy fell in love with her. Despite our long history together, I had become so disgusted with the dog that I was not upset to see the people take her away to Waterford, a hick town several miles east of Modesto. I have to admit that when Livy and the people were gone it seemed too easy for us to get rid of a dog we'd had for so long. And it was. The people called the next day and said their landlord wouldn't let them have the dog. Luckily, we were still getting calls on the ad in the paper, and soon there was another family at the house meeting Livy. I don't remember what lie we told when they asked us why we wanted to give away a healthy, good-natured adult dog, but in any case they, too, fell in love with Livy and took her home. And we waited for the phone to ring.

We didn't get the call as soon as we expected and it wasn't exactly the call we thought would come, but several days later the phone rang. It wasn't the people who had taken Livy home. No, that would be too easy and obvious. Instead, when Paula answered the phone, the person calling said, "We found your dog." I was just a third party listening to one side of the conversation, but I was nonetheless able to get the gist of the discussion. Predictably, Livy had escaped from her new owners, and the callers had found her and fallen in love. Apparently, they had no previous beagle experience. They called us because the dog still had on the tags with our number. I started contributing to the call through Paula's other ear: "We don't have a dog. That dog is not lost. Of course she's friendly. Please remove the nametag with our number on it. Yes, by all means, you can keep her."

Paula, though, felt compelled by some pet code of ethics to contact the people who had taken her home from us to let them know the dog had been found and taken into protective custody. Their response went something like, "Let the other people keep the damned dog. There is no yard that can contain that dog." It turns out they were interested in dog ownership—not dog rental or dog inn keeping, which is all you can hope for with a wandering hound. So Livy went to stay (I use the term loosely) with her third adoptive family. Although her new family lived in an area not far from our house, we never saw any sign of Livydog again.

As I said before, I had grown so tired of her disappearing act that I felt no sadness at the time to see her go (forever). But now, looking back, I realize that there's something wrong with not seeing a dog through its entire natural life—however long or short it might be. If Livy were still alive today (it's conceivable, but unlikely), she would be sixteen, going on seventeen. I suppose, though, because we didn't keep her until the bitter end, she remains for me the incredible Houndini—always escaping, always lighting out.

Longball

In the summer of 1990, I started playing softball with other people (mostly men, a few women) from the English department at SIU in a standing pick-up game at the ball field behind Unity Point School, just south of town on US 51. It wasn't exactly a pick-up game because the teams were basically set every week: under 30s versus over 30s. Faculty, graduate students, and even a few undergraduates played, and the thirty–year-old cut off insured that the game was essentially faculty against graduate students.[54] People could be shifted from one team to another to even

---

[54] Novelist and future Pulitzer-Prize winner Richard "Rick" Russo and acclaimed poet Rodney Jones were among the regular faculty players, and thus many of the graduate students who participated in the softball game were enrolled in the

out the sides, but never any key personnel. Players showed up at the school at noon every Saturday, weather and field conditions permitting, but those who came a little early could take some batting practice to loosen up. During the games, nobody kept track of the number of innings we played; we played until the oldest man on the field, Dick Lawson, called out "last inning!" as he took his position on the pitcher's mound. The old team, which tended to play station-to-station on offense and conservatively on defense, almost always won. The young team was capable of individual heroics, but we played sloppily. It didn't help that Dick wouldn't call last inning until the old guys had the lead. On those rare Saturdays when we won, I can remember getting six or seven at-bats before they finally called it a game.

I had heard there was a group that played softball on Saturdays soon after we arrived on campus in August of 1989, but I didn't know anyone and Paula didn't know anyone because she wasn't in the graduate program yet. And I didn't want to take off for two or three hours on a Saturday afternoon after she had been working all week at the Copy Shop. I wasn't encouraged to go out and play when I saw my fellow graduate students playing a game at the fall department picnic. I remember someone hit a pop up. And as the infielders converged on the ball and the first baseman

---

department's creative writing program. The student writers liked to play poker, drink beer, and smoke on Friday nights and then play ball on Saturday afternoons.

staggered underneath it, a player on the batter's team yelled out, "It's perplexing!" I thought to myself—these people play like English majors.

Eventually, one of the faculty players heard about my baseball past and suggested I come out and play. I was assured that the games were actually competitive and fun. When I showed up at the field, no one paid much attention to the fact that I was there, until I stepped into the left side of the batter's box to take some B. P. I felt a little rusty, but I lined the second pitch off the bottom of the right field fence, which I immediately discovered was a rather short porch. Suddenly, I was the new kid in town, and the young team was infused with a little hope. During that first game, I hit a fly ball off the end of the bat to straightaway right. As I jogged to first base, I was shocked as the right fielder ran out of room and the ball cleared the fence for my first Unity Point home run. As I rounded the bases, Lee Person, who was playing third base, said, "Nice hit." I was embarrassed that the ball had gone out and I didn't want to act like I had hit some prodigious blast. So I said to Lee, "That was a piece of crap home run." He shrugged, and the game went on. But I realized that instead of sounding embarrassed, I made myself look like a cocky jackass, who had hit so many home runs I could afford to be picky.

My comment bugged me so much that I went in to Lee's office on Monday and apologized for sounding obnoxious. He was cool about it, but I assured him that I didn't make a habit of popping off to my fellow players and opponents. My next home run, in the next game, was much more satisfying. I hit it off a guy named Earl. Earl was a graduate student who weaseled his way on to the old team whenever he could, especially when Dick Lawson missed a game and wasn't there to pitch for them.[55] In the week since my first homer, I had time to reflect on my hitting strategy. I decided I was just going to pull everything, get the ball up in the air, and shoot for the short Unity Point fence. So in my first at-bat against Earl, I got right up on the plate to take away the outside corner. But Earl was a clever bastard, and he saw that I was crowding the plate. Instead of pitching me away, he tossed one off the inside corner. I turned on it, and I hit it a country mile. Unfortunately, I hooked it a little, and as the ball flew over the fence it was five or ten feet foul. There were a few oohs and aahs from players on both teams, and Earl said something like, "There's strike one."

It took a few minutes for someone to run down the game ball beyond the fence, so I had a minute to strategize further. I realized that I did not have to get full extension on my swing or swing with all my might to reach the fence. I got back into the batter's box,

---

[55] Earl liked to play with the old guys because (1) he liked to be on the winning side and (2) he lived to suck up. I don't know whatever happened to Earl, but I don't dare mention his last name because he undoubtedly would sue for libel. Once, he actually tried to maneuver and manipulate the election of officers in our little English graduate student organization, attempting in the process to keep me from becoming the organization's chairperson.

hoping Earl would try to jam me one more time. He did, and this time when I turned on it I shortened my swing—like Tiger Woods hitting a stinger 3-wood. The ball actually carried farther than the previous one (because it didn't have as much topspin), and it flew straight as a string, fair by at least twenty feet. I don't remember if we won or lost that day (we probably lost), but I do know that from that day forward I tried to hit a homer every time I came to bat.

Thus began my two-year course of study in dinger sciences. I had played ball all my life, but I was never a home run hitter. When I played baseball (I was just good enough to play briefly in college), I was a left-handed junkball pitcher. I also played some fast-pitch softball, but I was mostly a Punch-and-Judy kind of hitter (which is not uncommon in fast-pitch).[56] Then when I played slow-pitch, I played on mostly lower-division teams where home runs are discouraged (and sometimes prohibited) by three hundred-foot fences and restricted-flight balls. On the other hand, upper division (A, B, and some C) games are often boring affairs. A typical inning goes like this: the first two batters milk out walks, and then the third batter, who is likely a 6'4" 250lb. ex-linebacker, hits one 350 feet. I know it doesn't fit most people's idea of slow-pitch softball, but the competitive lower-division teams on which I played depended on

---

[56] Except for the women's game, fast-pitch softball has all but disappeared, which is a shame because it's a great game of pitching, defense, and situational hitting.

fundamentals. We turned double plays, hit cut off men, went first to third on bloop singles, and even hit behind the runner.

Like most guys who come to slow-pitch from baseball, I always grabbed the biggest, heaviest bat I could find. My thinking was that the heavy bat would compensate for two things: (1) my inability to be patient and wait for the pitch to get to the plate, and (2) the lack of power supplied by the pitcher. However, when I started playing at Unity Point, I tried a 34-inch, 32-ounce "Black Magic" model bat that was owned by an older graduate student named Jim.[57] I think Jim and I were the only people to use the Black Magic, but it seemed to have a large sweet spot and the ball just jumped off it when I hit with it. I discovered that all the power I needed to hit the ball over the short fence was located above my knees and below my shoulders. For once in my life, my thick thighs and ample stomach were being put to good use.

As I mentioned before, my approach was to crowd the plate as much as I could. In fact, I wanted the pitch to come right at me. The perfect pitch to hit, in my mind, was one that would hit me if I didn't swing at it. As the pitch approached, I turned my hips and stomach open toward the right field line while keeping my hands back and relaxed. Then I put a hard but short swing on the ball, concentrating only on hitting the ball with the barrel of the bat. The

---

[57] In slow-pitch, I had never used anything lighter than a 34-ounce bat. Jim was not the bat owner's real name. I will mention him later, and it will be obvious why I am not using his name.

power, as I said, came from my mid-section, not my arms, shoulders, or hands. Because I didn't need to extend my arms or roll my wrists over, I could let the ball get closer to me before swinging. And my hits didn't hook toward the foul line.[58]

The exhilaration of hitting one out of the ballpark, even a tiny place like the Unity Point field, is intoxicating, and I quickly became addicted. Each at-bat was a little drama that began with Dick Lawson telling his defense to shift. Three of the four outfielders lined up along the fence in right field. The second baseman, usually Rodney Jones (winner of the Book Critics Circle Award for Poetry), dropped back into short right field, and the shortstop moved behind second base. The shift inevitably led someone on my own team to say something about trying to hit one to the left side where no one was standing. I ignored this advice.[59] Dick then tried to get me to swing at a pitch that was either over my head or short of the plate. There were no bases on balls in our friendly game, so I could not be intentionally walked. On one hand, this rule meant Dick could just keep tossing one bad pitch after another, but at the same time I could just stand there until I got

---

[58] From around 1999 to 2004, Barry Bonds used essentially this same technique, combined with incredible natural quickness and chemically aided strength, to hit many, many home runs.

[59] I see now that this refusal to go the other way might not have endeared me to my teammates. In all the games I played over the next two years, I hit one ball to the opposite field. Because of the defensive shift to the other side of the field, the ball rolled from the edge of the outfield grass down the left field line all the way to the fence. I got a triple. Homers are better.

something fat to hit. Fortunately, neither of us was interested in playing that way, and normally I put the ball in play by the second or third pitch, which was the climax of the drama. Only the conclusion varied.

I usually knew on contact if the ball was going over the fence, so I became accustomed to admiring the ball's flight from the batter's box and then trotting gingerly (like the Babe himself) around the bases. I'm not particularly proud of this behavior, but as I said I was addicted to the thrill and I wanted to savor it. After all, if you crank one and go tearing down the first base line, you might miss something—like how far or how high the ball travels. I have no idea how many times I went deep between 1990 and 1992, but I can count on one hand the number of games in which I did not homer. Two home runs a game was probably my typical performance, but three was not out of the question. Once, one glorious Saturday, I hit four balls out of the park. The reason I hit four was that the young team was ahead, and the old guys wouldn't give up. So we kept playing, and I kept getting at-bats, probably six or seven, and I kept connecting. One of the homers was a grand slam, and our team scored something like eighteen runs in a nine or ten-inning game. I had maybe ten runs batted in.

This particular game occurred during a slight upturn in the young team's fortunes, much of which was due to the fact that I started bringing my friend Doug Emanus to the games with me. It was understood that the game was for people associated with the English department, but friends were "okay" when we needed people to fill out the teams. Doug more than filled out our team. He played a solid short stop, which in turn allowed us to move another decent player to the outfield with me. To their credit, the old team mostly let this violation of the rules slide—unless there were more than enough players (or we won too often).

About a year and a half after I started playing on Saturdays, tragedy struck. My beloved "Black Magic" bat left town with its owner, who had run into problems with his comprehensive exams and run out of time with his assistantship.[60] I couldn't justify, either to myself or to my wife, spending $50 on my own Black Magic, so I went to Wal-Mart and bought a look-a-like for $12.96.[61] The new bat, which I'll call Curtis, was the same length, weight, and diameter as Black Magic, so I thought I would give it a try. Curtis worked well enough. I could still routinely hit the ball over the fence at Unity Point with Curtis, but the bat lacked, well, magic. I might

---

[60] The comprehensive exam is the most intimidating and downright scary requirement for the PhD. In our program, candidates sat for twelve hours (over three days) of essay exams—six hours the first day and three the second and third days. Failing the exams basically meant no dissertation and no degree.

[61] It's important to note here that I no longer shop at Wal-Mart. At the time, Wal-Mart still claimed to buy and sell American whenever and wherever possible. My new bat may have been made in China, but at least I could still find a T-shirt or a pair of jeans made in the USA. Today, I don't begrudge any poor person who shops at Wal-Mart out of necessity, but Wal-Mart has done more to insure that that poor person stays poor than George W. Bush, Dick Cheney, Tom De Lay, Ken Lay, ExxonMobil, McDonald's, and the Grinch who stole Christmas.

sound picky, but my home runs with Curtis just weren't as prodigious as they were with Black Magic, which meant I couldn't always just stand there and admire the ball's flight over the fence. I still have Curtis. I keep it under our bed. Long since retired from active duty, Curtis lies ready to protect the family against intruders.

I realize that I might have, so far, given the impression that I was the Babe Ruth of Unity point, hitting more home runs than all the other players combined. Actually, there were a number of players who could hit the long ball. A few of my teammates on the young team were capable. A young guy named Bill, a budding short story writer, was a good player, and he hit homers occasionally. Doug Emanus hit one or two when he played with us. And I should mention my friend Karl, who once accused me of hitting a softball farther than I could hit a golf ball. On the old side, the owner of Black Magic, Jim, could hit the ball out, and Lee Person, whom I mentioned earlier, knocked a few homers.[62] I remember Rick Russo once hit a "walk-off" grand slam that stole a win from the young team. Rick left SIU to go to Colby College in Maine, and on the last day he played with us we had to move to another field in town because Unity Point was too wet. We ended up playing on a grass field (I think it was the outfield of a baseball diamond) without a

---

[62] Lee, by the way, is a well-known American literature scholar, and he served on both my exam and dissertation committees.

backstop or fences. At the end of the day, we all signed a ball and gave it to Rick. I'm sure he treasures it to this day.

By far, the leading power hitter for the predominantly faculty team was David Blakesley, a young, fairly big rhetorician from California. David, who was an expert in the theories of Kenneth Burke and Mikhail Bakhtin, was a threat to go deep every time he came to bat. His hitting style, though, was completely the opposite of mine. David stood off the plate and liked to get his arms fully extended. Whereas I was a dead pull, left-handed, line-drive hitter, David, a right-handed hitter, was capable of hitting the ball out of the park in any direction. He hit soaring fly balls that were just as likely to go over the right field fence as the left field fence. David won many games for the old team, but I wouldn't say we were rivals at all. Nobody kept track of who hit more home runs, or anything like that. David missed a game one time, and that particular day I hit a ball that seemed to be still gaining speed and altitude when it left the yard. The ball flew directly over one of the outfielders stationed in right field. The fielder, whose back was literally against the fence, made no move to catch the ball because it was at least 15 feet over his head as it went over the fence. Later the next week, another graduate student and I were telling David about the game he had missed, and the other student said, "You should have seen this home run Dan hit. It was just a straight line drive." David said something like, "What do you mean? All of Dan's homers are line drives." And he was right. I lacked variety.

* * *

I had to kick my homer habit when we moved to Springfield in August of 1992. I was in Carbondale during the week throughout the fall, but not on the weekend. We had only one occasion to be in Carbondale on a Saturday in October. Our friends, Doug and Anna, had something going on (I don't remember what), and we came in to town to see them. We stayed in a cheap motel between Carbondale and Murphysboro. Somehow, it worked out that I had Saturday afternoon free (and I had brought my glove and Curtis along), so I went out to see if the game was on. The weather had started to turn cool and the school was in the middle of a three-day weekend, so I discovered that only a handful of players had come out to play. We were short fielders and we didn't have a decent game ball, but we played anyway. The air was heavy and a little damp, and the old ball we used didn't want to fly. I bounced a few balls off the wall, but there were no homers that day, for anyone. When we all got tired, we quit, and I went back to the motel to catch up with Paula.

I never went out to Unity Point again. My reign as longball king ended quietly with no fanfare (no signed ball from my compatriots). The next spring I found a local Springfield team on which to play, but my homering days were over.[63] I have no idea if the standing Saturday afternoon game at Unity Point School is still standing. I do know that the student population is always evolving, and most of the faculty who played when I did have either retired or moved on to other universities. Richard Peterson (the department chair), Rodney Jones, and Dick Lawson made those games possible and I hope that there have been new ball-playing faculty who have followed in their cleat steps.

Postscript: I recently ran into Karl, mentioned above, at an academic conference, and our conversation quickly turned to the old softball days. Karl, who is now an editor at the SIU press, let me know that the weekly games eventually died out. I apologize for throwing a wet blanket on the somewhat sentimental ending of the piece.

---

[63] The fences in Springfield were too far and high, and the balls used weren't very lively. I actually hit two (I think) inside-the-park homers in Springfield when I hit hard liners that the right fielders misjudged and then misplayed.

The World is My Urinal: a Frank Discussion

What I have learned in my many years as a keen observer of human nature and western civilization is that the one thing that comes between men and women is the urinal, or rather the ability to use a urinal. The official female view of the urinal is that it is an abomination of modern plumbing, a convenience that reveals the true barbaric and indiscreet nature of the male of the species. At least that's the response I get whenever I suggest that if we ever (which means never) get to build a custom home, I'm going to put a urinal in the master bathroom. Instead of seeing the benefits of the home urinal (which are many, by the way), Paula thinks of it as a strange, dirty fixture of public restrooms.[64]

For males, the urinal becomes a kind of given, an accepted part of the public landscape, soon after we get big enough to go to the restroom by ourselves. We learn the procedures, protocols, and the techniques as young boys, and then we give the process very little conscious attention—unless one encounters a really unusual situation. But I'm the only male in my household, and I'm always amused by the reaction of my wife and daughters to even the sight of a urinal. Let's say there's a men's room scene in a movie we're watching and the camera catches a glimpse of a urinal. They look at it in wonder and repulsion. There have been times when we've been traveling and I've tried to convince the girls or Paula just to use the men's room when there's no one else around, so that we could all go more quickly. Besides the assumption that it will be disgusting, what stops them from using the men's room is the fear that there might actually be a urinal in there.

I think some women are downright resentful of the urinal. These women believe that the urinal is part of our culture's conspiracy to keep women down. From what I gather, this theory holds that if you have a mixed group of business people or co-

---

[64] The home urinal would (1) eliminate the age-old toilet seat up or down battle; (2) contribute to a cleaner toilet, toilet area, and bathroom environment; and (3) allow for more efficient use of the facilities (there's a reason your line is always longer, ladies.).

workers, and they all went to the bathroom, the men could walk into the bathroom together, walk up to their respective urinals together, do their business together, and, all the while, never stop doing business together. On the other hand, the women, who would probably be outnumbered anyway, would be cut off from the continued business dealings of the men in the men's room and from each other because they do their business in the relative privacy of a stall. I have to admit the idea looks pretty good on paper, and the notion that men actually get further ahead in the world because they're willing (and able) to pee like animals is a subject worthy of a dissertation in any number of academic disciplines. However, I am nothing if not an enlightener of society and a bridger of the gender gap, so I want to shed the light of truth on this subject. Men don't chat at the urinal. Those who do are weirdos who probably have trouble in other social areas. Maybe it's because it is hard to converse when you are looking straight ahead, and if you talk you might accidentally turn your head toward the other guy. Or, maybe it's because we're preoccupied with the purpose of our visit to the bathroom.

      This alleged conspiracy prevents me from getting my home urinal. It stands to reason that if the urinal is a symbol of public, male-dominated space, the domestic bathroom must remain safely within feminine jurisdiction. A urinal in the home would be an intrusion or even a violation of female space. Men are allowed to use the home bathroom as a courtesy—to keep them from going on the lawn (hold that thought for later). If I put a urinal in the bathroom at home, it would mean that I had a claim, however partial, to that space. So we (Paula and I, men and women) have an arrangement, one that is a fundamental, albeit unspoken, social compact: urinals stay out of homes and men retain the advantage of urinating like animals.

Upon further reflection, I have decided that I am okay with the deal. Peeing like an animal is a skill I would not like to forfeit because when I go standing up it means that the world is my urinal. And when the world is your urinal, you can go in some mighty fine places. I'd like to illustrate this point with brief descriptions and discussions of the three best places I have ever gone, two of which I discovered while Paula and I were living in the Midwest.

* * *

Between 1990 and 1993, Paula and I managed to go to old Busch Stadium in St. Louis two or three times when the San Francisco Giants came to town. In 1993, the Giants opened their season in St. Louis against the Cardinals. We were able to get tickets to the second (I think) game of the series. The Giants lost the game, but Barry Bonds, who had left the Pittsburgh Pirates in the off-season, homered for the first time as a Giant. My fondest memory of Busch Stadium, though, has nothing to do with any of the games we saw there. What I remember most vividly is my first trip to the men's room. As I entered the bathroom, what I noticed initially was the sound of Jack Buck's perfectly raspy voice coming through the speakers in the ceiling. Then I saw a row of one gleaming white urinal after another. Further, the men's room was clean and climate controlled. It all added up to a delightful environment in which to pee.

I grew up going to ballgames (once or twice a year) at the Oakland-Alameda County Coliseum (home of the Athletics and Raiders) and Candlestick Park in San Francisco (home of the Giants and 49ers). The men's rooms at the Coliseum and Candlestick had all the charm of a Turkish prison cell. They were like indoor cattle pens: dirty, smelly, dim, and ill-equipped. Instead of urinals, the bathrooms featured long pee troughs in front of which men and boys stood shoulder-to-shoulder and peed as quickly as possible. When the restrooms were busy the only personal space at the pee trough was inside your own head, and as you shuffled forward in your line, your only hope was that when your time came there wouldn't be any stage fright. The trough, as one might imagine, was disgusting. There was only one drain at the center of each trough, and there was only a constant trickle of fresh water piped in from the wall to "flush" the trough out. Any normal human being didn't dare look around or down, even when zipping up. Sadly, many patrons responded to the sub-human conditions by behaving like sub-humans—which just made the restrooms even more dreadful. Compared to Oakland and San Francisco, the good folks at Busch Stadium had created a veritable Taj Mahal of toilets. And even though I've since been to other ballparks with fine facilities (including the Giants' new Pacific Bell/SBC/AT&T Park) and old Busch has been replaced by new Busch, that first men's room remains one of the three best places I have ever gone.

As rewarding as the Busch restroom experience was, it places a distant third to my number-two spot to pee—our front porch. I explained in "Houndini" that in 1990 we moved to a place out in the country, and the front door of our duplex faced nothing but soybeans. I did not mention, though, that the duplex had two bedrooms and one bathroom (actually, we never had two bathrooms until we bought our house in 1996). If you have one bathroom and you live in town, or you're somewhat civilized, or you are a woman, you have no choice but to wait in line for the facilities. Fortunately, none of these descriptions applied to me at the time. So, many times when my lovely wife occupied the bathroom and nature called, I stepped out to the edge of nature and let nature take its course. Our front porch was elevated about two feet above the lawn, and it was a steady downhill run for about twenty feet to the edge of the soybean field. I usually slipped back into the house and washed my hands in the kitchen without Paula suspecting anything.

I know a small percentage (perhaps 50-90%) of readers might find my behavior inappropriate. Those same readers might also say that my outdoor urination simply reinforces the idea that men are pigs. To those disapproving individuals, I would point out that I peed off the porch only under the cover of night. The complete darkness prevented anyone who might have been out there from seeing me. When I stood out there with the porch light off, it felt like I was a hundred miles from civilization.[65] But I suppose if you're peeing outdoors, from the edge of your front porch, you've already said goodbye to civilization. Frankly, civilization has its own problems, too, and if peeing outdoors or in the woods is wrong according to civilization, then I don't want to be right.

Sadly, I'll never be able to go again at old Busch or the duplex on Rural Route 3, but I think of them now and again, especially when I get to take a leak at the best place I've ever gone—a place I call Schoolhouse Ridge. Schoolhouse Ridge, as the name implies, runs along the top of a mountain. It's not a tall mountain (actually one could call it a hill), and it sits at an elevation of only 3,000 feet above sea level in the foothills of the Sierra Nevada Mountains. The ridge is only accessible by ATV, dirt bike, or Jeep (though we've never seen one up there). The trail that leads

---

[65] Actually, during the summer, we never opened the front door with the porch light on because there were flying insects the size of Chihuahuas (and almost as annoying) that would swarm the porch as soon as the light came on. Many of these bugs looked like the ridiculous medals you see hanging from the military uniforms of South American dictators.

up to the ridge, as one might imagine, is rough, rocky, and rutted, and it can only be found if the rider knows where to turn off from a larger fire road. There is only one way in and one way out. I would be happy to provide a fuller description of the ridge's exact location, but my fellow hillbillies have sworn me to secrecy. I will reveal, though, that depending on which route we use to get to the Schoolhouse turn-off, it can take us up to an hour of riding to get there from base camp. So when we reach the ridge, just about everyone needs to take a leak, except for my brother-in-law Ritch, whom I like to call "the camel."

We call it "Schoolhouse Ridge" because when we first discovered it, we found several school desks, the kind used in high school or college, on top of the ridge at the end of the trail. I don't know for sure why the desks were left there, though it seems reasonable that the hill could have been used once as a fire lookout. Because we don't have the means to carry the desks down the hill on our quads and bikes, the desks have remained there, gradually disintegrating, over the years. The hill is covered in manzanita and other scraggly vegetation. There may be a few scrub oaks here and there, but on top of the ridge there is nothing to obstruct the view. And Schoolhouse is all about the view. To the south and down the hill, we can see highway 140 and the Merced River snaking its way down to the central valley. To the west and north, there are seemingly endless hills and ravines. And to the east, well…the east is priceless. Schoolhouse Ridge affords an unobstructed view all the way (maybe fifteen to twenty miles) to Yosemite Valley. Half Dome (on the right) and El Capitan (on the left) stand guard over the valley, and they seem to hold back the even higher peaks beyond them. There are days when we can see forever into the high country, but other times the peaks are shrouded in clouds and we can only feel their presence.

When I answer nature's call on top of Schoolhouse Ridge in plain view of Half Dome and El Capitan, I can't help but feel that the world is indeed my urinal.

Boxcar Willie; Or, How I Stopped Worrying and Learned to Love the Buffet

[Author's note: Before I begin a story about Branson, Missouri and its musical attractions, I need to reveal that I grew up a fan of <u>Hee Haw</u>. In fact, I can still recite some of their old corn-pone comedy bits. Thus, in case the reader expected the piece to exude a sarcastic, belittling tone (from the perspective of an educated social critic), let me say. . .well, you're right. That's exactly what it is. But it's not because I'm a snob.]

P aula and I first visited Branson, Missouri, while we were living in Carbondale. Paula's paternal grandparents, Hurd and Marge Barrington, traveled east from California on an RV trip, and they got as far as Missouri. They wanted to see us, but we'd have to make the trip to Branson. When

Hurd and Marge arrived at an RV park just south of Branson, Hurd tried calling us to let us know they had made it there. Unfortunately, we were not home to answer the phone, and our answering machine picked up. At the time, Paula and I had put a Hans and Franz (from *Saturday Night Live*) greeting on the answering machine:

"I am Dan."

"I am Paula."

(together) "And we are not here to pump you up!"

(me) "So leave your name and number, and we'll call you back…Maybe."

The message concluded with a few seconds of derisive Teutonic laughter. Most people who called and got the machine thought the message was hilarious. Paula's grandpa thought that he had called some lunatics and didn't leave a message. Luckily, he called back later when Paula was home, and we made plans to go see them for the weekend.

We took the scenic route (surprise) from Carbondale to Branson, which led us through the northern part of the Ozarks and certainly prepped us for a hillbilly weekend. In addition to camping spaces, the RV park offered rustic cabins, and Paula's grandparents had reserved one for our lodging for the weekend. We arrived on a Friday evening, and Hurd and Marge informed us that we would all be attending a music show the next afternoon. We were going to see one of the two original Branson shows, the Presley Country Jubilee (the other is called the Baldknobbers). By 1990, business was already booming in Branson. New splashy and flashy music theaters were being built along Highway 76, the main drag through town, and all around the area. The music lovers who were attracted to these theaters must get very hungry because we found that Branson also featured a plethora of casual dining establishments, most of which had the words "country" and "buffet" in their names.[66]

The nice thing about the Presley show is that audiences were treated (and I assume they still are) to fairly authentic hillbilly music and hillbilly humor. It could be said that in Branson they play both kinds of music: country and western. But that old joke doesn't tell the whole story of the Branson musical buffet. The music tourists who come to Branson from the Midwest and the west, in addition to the south, are in their fifties, sixties, and seventies. And they seem to be less concerned with the genre of the music than the era of the music—which is why performers (or "singers," if you prefer) like Wayne Newton, Tony Orlando, and Andy Williams have tried their luck in Branson.

---

[66] As far as I can tell, Branson was conceived of as a place where white people could gather in peace and homogeneity to celebrate their unique white culture, which consists of country music and country-fried steak—not that there's anything wrong with that. Some of my best friends are white people. Despite all the negative stereotypes, I have found that once you get to know them, white people aren't all that different.

In most Branson theaters, the audience is fed a steady diet of easy-listening country music from the 1950s, 60s, and 70s. Those performers who actually had hits play them, and those who didn't have hits play the hits of other people. There's a Branson phenomenon I have never seen elsewhere (but maybe it happens in other places, too. I haven't been everywhere.). I think we are all familiar with the custom of an audience giving a courtesy clap (something like a gallery clap in golf) when they hear a singer or band start playing one of their classic hits. The singer will often give the audience some little acknowledgement of the audience's appreciation: a nod, a bow, even a pause. But in Branson, the audiences often give the courtesy clap to singers who aren't singing their own songs. And the singers accept the applause as if the music was their own creation. For instance, let's say Boxcar Willie launches into Johnny Cash's "Folsom Prison Blues." The audience hears a song they recognize and like, so they applaud as if Boxcar Willie were responsible in some way for this piece of music. Boxcar Willie then graciously nods to the audience's approval. It's bizarre, and it's musical plagiarism. In Branson, though, authenticity and originality often take a back seat to familiarity and availability. In fact, those two qualities (familiarity and availability), along with a third, affordability (some would call it value), are the key ingredients to Branson's popularity. And it's no coincidence that familiarity, availability, and affordability are what make buffet restaurants popular, especially with the typical Branson customer. In other words, the music in Branson is a lot like the food at a buffet restaurant: the customer knows what it is, there is a lot of it, and it is fairly inexpensive.

As I intimated earlier, I actually liked the music at the Presley theater. Even though the headliners in Branson are cheesy has-beens, the musicians who work there are often top-notch professionals, with many doing studio work in Nashville and Los Angeles. The Presley players showed range and talent, to go along with their hillbilly sensibility. The show moved briskly through its two hours until the big finale, at which point the entire cast gathered on stage to sing Lee Greenwood's "I'm Proud to be an American." As the group sang the song, a low-resolution video projection of an American flag filled the entire backdrop of the stage. The audience responded by standing and singing along. Many (most really) put their hands over their hearts or saluted, as if the band were playing "The Star-Spangled Banner" or reciting the Pledge of Allegiance. Paula looked at me as we got out of our seats (hey, we didn't want to be attacked by the 400 senior citizens all around us), and her face clearly said, "Where are we?"

I figured this one visit to Branson with Hurd and Marge would be enough to last a lifetime. However, when we moved to Springfield (which is only forty-five minutes north of Branson) in 1992, we began to receive a steady stream of visitors from the west coast, all of whom were determined to experience Branson. In three years in Carbondale, we had only two visitors from California. My mother came to see us once, and so did Paula's mom.[67]

Our first Springfield visitors were Paula's mom, Lynda, and her beloved Grandma Bea. They came to see Paula receive her MA from SIU and to help us settle into our little house on N. Elmwood Avenue. But of course we had to go to Branson and take in a show. We went to a theater that was called the Grand Palace (I think), and we saw a double-bill matinee performance by Glen Campbell and Waylon Jennings. Waylon's musical wife, Jessie Coulter, also sang a song or two during his set. The show was enjoyable enough because both Glenn and Waylon had a decent catalogue of their own hits to play and, because it was a double bill, neither played too long. On the other hand, neither man seemed overly enthused about singing at 2:00 pm to an auditorium that was two-thirds full of Paula, me, and few hundred AARP members.

About a month later, my dad's cousin, Clara, and her husband, Wilton (also called Mike), came to see us. They were on a long trip with their travel trailer. They were able to park their trailer along our long driveway and stay a few days. Actually, they stayed with us a little while, and then they moved on to see Wilton's old

---

[67] We had one other visitor, Paula's second cousin, who was stationed at an Air Force base in Missouri. He came for a day. By the way, when Paula's mom visited, we drove through Kentucky down to Tennessee, and we went to both Nashville and Memphis. We took in both the Grand Ole Opry and Graceland.

navy buddy who lived in a small town near the Oklahoma-Missouri border. They stayed with the old buddy for several days, and then they went to an RV park down by Branson (I don't remember if it was the same RV park where Paula's grandparents stayed). While Wilton and Clara were camped in our driveway, we made our first trip to Silver Dollar City, an amusement park located just outside Branson.

Silver Dollar City features an old west or pioneer theme, and it is probably the only amusement park in the country built on an underground cavern, called Marvel Cave. Silver Dollar City has fun, if not death-defying, rides. For some reason, Wilton, Paula, and I decided to try their unique water ride (I don't remember what it is called) that is part-log ride, part-water slide, part-luge, and part-roller coaster. I've never ridden anything quite like it. First, we had to hike up I don't know how many steps to get to the top of the start tower. When we got to the top, we saw that the ride's "cars" were long, heavy mats that slid or floated freely through the ride's spiraling tubes. The ride's attendant directed us (three full-sized adults) onto a mat with a kid who was about twelve years old. The mats were brought up to the start tower on a conveyor, but once the four of us got on the mat it was all gravity all the way to the bottom. There were no seatbelts, only handles carved into the rubber mats. With perhaps 600 hundred pounds of flesh on top of it and an inch of water beneath it, that mat used every bit of the enclosed tube. We carried so much speed and weight into the corners that in the middle of each one we were turned completely sideways at a 90-degree angle. I realize that this was the basic idea, or desired effect, of the ride, but with our full load we were pushing the envelope.[68] I will never forget the look on Wilton's face when we got off that ride. I had never seen Wilton, who was in his late fifties at the time, at a loss for words. He was always quick with a joke or a story, but at that moment he was speechless.

Today, if I were compelled by some outside force (Homeland Security perhaps) to go to Branson and visit at least one attraction, I would go to Silver Dollar City. If I were forced to see one of the musical shows, I would take some consolation in the fact that I wouldn't have to see Boxcar Willie perform—because as I understand that he's dead. Unfortunately, when we lived in Springfield, he wasn't dead. Willie was alive and making train sounds in his own Branson theater. When Wilton and Clara returned from his friend's place and camped outside Branson, they invited us to come see them and go see a show. They had already been to a few shows (Jim Stafford, Shoji Tabuchi), but they wanted to treat us to one to thank us for our hospitality when they first arrived. So we went down to the RV park on a Saturday, and

---

[68] In subsequent trips to Silver Dollar City, I rode this ride again with smaller people (children) as my co-passengers and there was never any comparison to that first ride.

Wilton informed us that the only tickets they could get (it was the busy season and a weekend) were for the Boxcar Willie show.

Boxcar Willie occupied a theater that had been used previously by another performer (I'm not sure which one) who had moved on to nicer and newer digs. The theater building was basically a metal warehouse with a gaudy façade. I don't recall much about the music in Willie's show, except that they played "The Orange Blossom Special" with Willie making train whistle sounds.[69] Like all Branson shows, this one incorporated humor throughout the performance. I remember Willie told a few jokes only a white audience would enjoy, and he made a few disparaging remarks about Hank Williams, Jr., which elicited shrugs and nods of agreement from the audience. Willie and one of his musicians performed an old vaudeville bit that's too long and complicated to describe here, but it ends in a punch line that asks, "What kind of a dog is it?" Any reader who recognizes this line will know the routine, and those who don't really don't need to care. The punch line, though, became a catch phrase around the house for a while. And if I saw Wilton and Clara tomorrow and I asked them "What kind of a dog is it?", they would get it.

Mostly, Boxcar Willie was interested in the up-sale. Yes, it only cost $12 (I'm guessing here) to get in the door, but the

---

[69] "The Orange Blossom Special" is played in Branson about as often as "I'm Proud to Be an American."

audience apparently needed to buy Boxcar Willie tapes, CDs, hats, shirts, coffee mugs, and, most of all, souvenir wooden train whistles. Most clever, though, was the sale of videotapes of the very performance the audience was attending. These videotapes were available immediately after the show, and Willie employed a number of savvy and unique sales techniques to encourage the audience members to purchase the tapes. First, the theater featured TV monitors (which were big enough for everyone to see) on either side of the stage so that the audience could see what was being taped. And what the people saw was themselves. Willie took the time to interact with the audience, which caused the video cameras to focus on the people watching the show. Even when Willie wasn't talking and joking with the audience, the cameras panned the crowd enough that everyone who attended the performance saw him or herself at least once on the monitors. Apparently, Boxcar Willie realized that very few people would be interested in taking home a video of The Boxcar Willie Show, but lots of people were willing to purchase a video of themselves *at* The Boxcar Willie Show. I still regret not buying that tape. After all, Willie talked directly to us (you're a sitting duck when you're thirty years younger than anyone else in the hall).

On the smorgasbord of the Branson musical buffet, Boxcar Willie wasn't exactly the roast beef or honey-baked ham, which attracts long lines of hungry customers. No, he was more like the three-bean salad down at the end of the table. The three-bean salad isn't anyone's first, second, or third choice, but as I suggested before it's familiar, there's plenty of it, and it's cheap.

Wilton and Clara visited early in the fall, the nicest time of the year in the region, and later in the fall it was my mother's turn to visit. She was fresh off a divorce from my dad, so a trip or two to Branson where we could spend a few hours in theaters and avoid conversation was just what this ABD ordered. My mom arrived around Thanksgiving and stayed maybe a week. At that time, the Branson attractions were moving closer to year-round operation, so many places were offering holiday productions. First, we took mom to Silver Dollar City where they had shifted from their "harvest" season to a holiday theme. Then we went to see Mel Tillis perform at the Mel Tillis Theater. If I remember correctly, Mel was one of the first big-name has-beens to move into Branson. His theater was nicely appointed and decorated for the season. Mel was definitely not on the three-bean salad end of the buffet. He was the fried chicken or even fried catfish, a popular staple but perhaps not the red meat.

We avoided Branson throughout the spring of 1993. I was finishing my dissertation and trying to find a real job. Paula was working full time and trying to get pregnant. And no one visited from California until the early summer, when Paula's Uncle Warren and Aunt Pat came to visit with their daughters, Allison and

Heather. The Carroll family was nearing the end of a cross-country vacation. They had flown from California to Washington, D.C., toured the historical sites in the area, and then rented a car and worked their way west to us in Springfield.[70]

We took the Carrolls to Silver Dollar City because we figured the girls would enjoy the rides and attractions there. By then, Paula was pregnant with our daughter Emily and couldn't ride the rides. Unfortunately, Warren and Pat had a definite idea about the music show they wanted to see. Apparently, they had been to Las Vegas many years before, and they had seen Wayne Newton's show. They loved it. And wouldn't you know it, Wayne was just then giving Branson a try in a brand-new theater. So the six of us went to The Wayne Newton Show. It was the best performance I have ever seen by a man wearing a girdle. Here's what I remember about Wayne's show: (1) Wayne perspired profusely, (2) Wayne performed a disturbing yet energetic rendition of Travis Tritt's "T-R-O-U-B-L-E," and (3) Wayne's skilled and talented back-up singers overwhelmed his painful warbling.

Going to see Wayne Newton in Branson was like going to Sizzler for the $9.95 steak and lobster, plus the all-you-can-eat salad and pasta bar. It seems like a great deal until you actually

---

[70] Uncle Warren's real name is Paul. Warren is his middle name. Paul was also his dad's name, so the family calls him Warren. When he took his family on this vacation, Warren was particularly interested in tourist sites related to Charles Carroll, one of the signers of the Declaration of Independence. Warren is fairly sure he's a descendant of the founding father.

experience it. For one thing, steak and lobster have no business being in a buffet restaurant. The premier items on a buffet should be either (a) slow-cooked and covered with barbeque sauce or (b) deep-fried. These often-delicious items can be properly prepared, without great danger of food poisoning, and offered in generous portions to the customer at an economical price.[71] On Branson's musical buffet table, Roy Clark, Jim Stafford, Ray Stevens, Mel Tillis, and others are all barbequed or deep-fried. One is about the same as the others, and that suits the Branson audience.[72] Consistency is king. Other audiences might want something exotic or unique (a little lobster or even steak), especially if you're going to several shows during one visit. But what if the steak is tough or the lobster gives you the trots? Is it worth the risk?

As far as I know (after all, I haven't been back), Wayne Newton failed to establish himself as a Branson mainstay—despite a splashy start. Branson visitors may not be picky, but they are smart enough not to pay $30 (or more) to see Wayne—with all his Vegas panache—do "T-R-O-U-B-L-E" when they can pay $15 to see the Presleys or the Balbknobbers do their own entertaining version of

---

[71] If the reader ever visits the Springfield area, I recommend Tiny's BBQ (I hope Tiny is still in business/alive) in order to experience these principles first hand. At several locations, Tiny's BBQ offers the best artery-clogging and tasty food in the area. Once, Paula and I saw the man himself, wedged into a corner booth, at one of his restaurants, counting his receipts from the lunchtime rush.

[72] I suppose previously unknown Japanese fiddle player Shoji Tabuchi, a Branson favorite, would have to be the exception that proves this rule. But I think he plays the same music as everybody else, so he would be like a Japanese buffet that serves deep-fried sushi.

the song. For all I know, Travis himself may have his own Branson theater by now.

The Carrolls were the last visitors we escorted to Branson. My mother and Paula's mom came again in August for my PhD graduation ceremony at SIU, but we didn't make a Branson trip. We were busy preparing to move to California. We obviously didn't see all the shows that the Branson musical buffet offered, but I don't think we missed all that much. And I say that in only a partially denigrating tone. What I mean is that we tasted enough items on the buffet to know what the whole buffet offered. No matter how many times we went back to see different performers, the experience would have been the same. I think I have mentioned this already, but we have never gone back to Branson. It's not a place from our past that we feel we need to show the kids, either. Somehow, though, I am glad it is in our past.

Workin' Man: Odd Jobs in a State of Misery

None of my friends or family would ever use the terms "workin' man" or "workaholic" to describe me. Now then, the judgments of these friends and relatives might be affected or influenced by a broader cultural perception of academia and the academics who inhabit it. But mostly people don't think I am a hard worker for good reason. In fact, there are times when I wish I could respond to my superiors and colleagues like Bartleby did in Herman Melville's story, "Bartleby the Scrivener." Of course, Bartleby kept saying "I prefer not to" all the way to the grave, so I do at least the minimum required of me to stay employed. Actually, I would say the key words in my relationship to work are "fear" and "loathing," as in my fear of unemployment is roughly equal to my loathing of employment. This standoff has kept me in the same position at the same institution for the last eleven years and will keep me there for another twenty (gasp). But as I said in the introduction to this book, it beats workin' for a livin'. And as Huck Finn would say, "I been there before."

* * *

We moved from Carbondale to Springfield, Missouri in August of 1992 because Paula secured a position as a full-time instructor in the English Department at Southwest Missouri State University (now called Missouri State University). Whereas I am terrible at getting hired, Paula can't miss. She finished her MA at SIU and applied for one job (at Southwest Missouri) and got it.[73] So we decided that we would move to Springfield, and I would complete my PhD at SIU from long distance. We couldn't afford for me to give up my teaching assistantship immediately, so for one semester (in the fall of 1992) I "commuted" from Springfield to Carbondale to teach two classes and work on my dissertation. I left our house early every Tuesday morning in our trusty Dodge Colt, drove the 300-plus miles to Carbondale, taught my two classes in the afternoon, crashed Tuesday night at Anna and Doug Emanus's

---

[73] When I was completing my PhD, I applied for probably 100 jobs and didn't get one interview.

house, worked at school all day Wednesday, stayed a second night at the Emanus house, taught my two classes again on Thursday afternoon, and drove to Springfield that evening.[74] I was usually home by 10:00 pm.

My return trip to Springfield often began with a stop at Quattro's Pizza in downtown Carbondale. Quattro's made the best pizza I have ever eaten, and they offered a great deal on a large one-item (pepperoni, of course) Chicago-style deep-dish and two large sodas.[75] I could call in the order from the office I shared with three other graduate assistants and then swing by the restaurant on my way out of town. Once the pizza and diet sodas were in the car with me, I would have a piece or two (and save the rest for when I got home to Paula) and drink the sodas. One time, though, I made a Quattro's run while I was in the middle of some dental work.[76] One of my two front teeth was wearing a temporary crown. When I was just outside of St. Louis, I took a big bite of still piping-hot pizza, and the thick cheese on top of the slice somehow wrapped around that temporary crown and pulled it off what was left of the real tooth. Now I knew right away something was wrong when the pizza

---

[74] I would like to say thank you to the kind folks in the English Department who gave me the convenient teaching schedule—which made the whole scheme possible.
[75] It's possible God created the Midwest just so there would be Chicago-style pizza.
[76] The best fringe benefit of Paula's job at Southwest Missouri was the fringe benefits. Our new medical and dental coverage allowed me to get some teeth work done, including the removal of wisdom teeth, and it made it possible for us to have Emily, our first born.

suddenly got crunchy. I pulled the crown out of my mouth, and when I saw what it was I instinctively and instantly looked up at my mouth in the rear-view mirror. There was my tooth stump in all its hillbilly glory. Despite the fact that I had already had crown and root canal work before, I had never actually seen what I glimpsed in the mirror. I looked like a character in a Branson music-variety show. I quickly inspected the temporary crown and then replaced it over the stump as best I could. Then I finished eating my slice.[77]

At the end of the fall semester I gave up my teaching assistantship and ended the regular commute. I applied for and received a tuition scholarship for the spring semester, and I only had to travel periodically to Carbondale to meet with my advisor, Dr. Ann-Janine (A-J) Morey. The scholarship covered my tuition, but I needed to generate some income to supplement Paula's salary. Because I needed the flexibility to take any given day off and I couldn't commit long-term to an employer, I signed up with a temporary employment agency. I had worked briefly as a male temp in California during one summer, so I knew what to expect—basically.

Let me say first that a male temporary worker is nothing like the proverbial Kelly Girl. Although I was willing and able to do office work, I was never sent out for an "inside" job. Instead, I shoveled sand, hung shelves, carried folding tables, moved furniture,

---

[77] This incident occurred at 65 miles per hour.

and pulled grommets (more on this one in a minute). During my temp work in the Springfield area, there were basically two kinds of employers: those who used temporary workers for one day to complete a specific job and those who regularly used temporary guys to do their normal business. These "regular" employers included a large local discount furniture store, a rental equipment business, and a General Electric manufacturing plant, and I spent many days toiling for each of these outfits. We all know that capitalism is based on the exploitation of the worker. The temporary business places two exploiters (the temp agency and the hiring firm) on the back of the worker. And the regular employers I just mentioned couldn't function without doubly exploited temps like me. Actually, they could do business without temps, but they knew that the temps maximized profits. So they dispensed with all but the most "essential" permanent staff, and chose to use the temp agency workers every day of the week (though the workers were rotated).

The G.E. plant, which I imagine has since been closed, was one of the company's last North American manufacturing sites. I think they kept it open because it was so low tech and their manufacturing costs were practically third world. The plant produced simple electric motors that could be used in a variety of industrial applications. The motors were attached to mounting brackets that allowed the motors to be installed in a number of positions. There were holes on every side of the bracket, and, depending upon the customer's order, grommets could be placed in whichever holes were necessary for the desired mounting position. Temporary workers were often called out to put the grommets in the holes. We were told which grommets were to be placed into which holes. We were given a pliers-like tool that was inserted through the hole. Then we put the grommet in the end of the tool and carefully pulled the tool back out of the hole so that the grommet would catch on either side of the bracket. Thus, the job was called "pulling grommets." And few of my life's meager accomplishment can compare with the feeling I got from successfully pulling hundreds of grommets in an eight-hour shift.

    I don't know how much money G.E. paid the temp agency for my efforts to help them bring good things to light, but it was the only job I was sent to in Springfield that paid the workers minimum wage, which at that time was four dollars and a shiny quarter per hour.[78] So in a full day of pulling grommets (with a ½ hour lunch), I could gross nearly $32. After one full day and maybe two half days at the G.E. plant, I declined to pull any more grommets (I don't remember if I said "I prefer not to"). Even though the work was mind-numbingly easy for a dexterous young man like me, it was not worth the time (anybody's time). I could take a shopping cart and

---

[78] Most jobs paid around $5 per hour.

go around town picking up cans and do better than $32, minus the taxes. To this day, I refuse to buy G.E. light bulbs or jet engines.[79]

Many states now have laws that allow employers to work people for over eight hours in one day without paying overtime, as long as the worker does not work more than forty hours for the week. In the state of misery, I mean Missouri, they've had this so-called "right-to-work" law for a long time, and there was one local furniture store that worked the system to perfection. They would bring out crews of temporary workers to unload, deliver, assemble, and set up furniture. A crew of workers would work two or three days, often for twelve or thirteen hours each day. It was not uncommon to work thirty-six hours in three days for $5 per hour. When one crew approached forty hours for the week, they were replaced by another crew.

A typical day working for the furniture store began at the warehouse, where we would unload semi-trailers and load furniture headed for the showroom into the delivery truck. Then we were shuttled over to the store, where we received instructions from the self-important salesmen. This store was not one where you select a piece of furniture and order it from the manufacturer. This place was a high-volume, "discount" retailer where you could buy furniture right off the showroom floor or from the store's own

---

[79] This statement is a lie.

warehouse.[80] When we arrived at the store, the salesmen always had a list of pieces that needed to be moved out, in, and around the showroom. Moving the mostly cheap furniture would not have been much of a task for a group of strong-backed young men if the showroom were not divided into display rooms. They had sample living rooms, family rooms, dining rooms, and bedrooms set up all around the big showroom and divided by partition walls. Thus, to get a sofa out of a spot by the front window, we had to take the scenic route through any number of "rooms," all the while holding the sofa high enough not to bump any of the other pieces. Once, I was passing through a dining room with a big sofa, and my partner and I were carrying it a good four inches above the oak table and chairs. Just as we were going by, a sales manager who looked like a poster child for angina hollered at us: "Lift it up! Lift it higher! It's gonna scratch. That's solid oak!" I'm glad I was in good shape at the time because I just looked over at the dude, shook my head, and lifted my end of the sofa about six inches higher. "We won't hit anything," I said.

Later in the afternoon, we often assembled furniture in the alley behind the store. Most of the kitchen tables, chairs, end tables, and coffee tables were delivered to the store disassembled in

---

[80] This store had a 'blowout" sale every week or so. I could walk into the store and see items marked closeout or clearance—after I had unloaded five more just like it that morning at the warehouse. One week a sofa would be listed at $750. The next week it would say $999 marked down to $799.

cardboard boxes. I hope the store's customers did not have to pay extra for our "professional" assembly because I'll confess right now that some of the screws and nuts and bolts didn't get fully tightened. In our defense, we were encouraged to work quickly and most of the time we had to use the flimsy tools included in the box with the furniture. Also in the afternoon, we loaded the delivery truck with the furniture we had pulled from the showroom. This furniture was moved to another warehouse where it awaited pick-up or home delivery. Once or twice, I was selected to help the delivery driver, who was just a kid, but he was the kid of someone who worked at the store. Twelve hours after we started, we were told we could call it a day. Somebody signed our time cards—accurate down to the ¼ hour—and we went home.

The rental outfit didn't pay any more than the furniture store, nor was the work any less strenuous. I nonetheless preferred to work there over any of the other regular employers. For one thing, the permanent employees, including the management, treated the temps, at least those who were responsible and hard working, humanely. More important, the work itself was a little more interesting—even though it often consisted of loading a truck full of folding tables, riding to a customer's site, unloading the tables, going to another site, picking up another set of tables, heading back to the warehouse, and unloading again. This routine may sound monotonous to anyone who has an interesting job, but not being stuck in one miserable location all day was a treat for a grunt like me. Besides, I became an expert at lifting, carrying, and stacking folding tables.

In the days just before and after July 4, 1993, I helped move what seemed like 10,000 tables. In Springfield, the sale and purchase of fireworks is illegal within the city limits. So the firework companies set up just beyond the outskirts of town on any vacant piece of land they could find and rent. They did not build little wooden shacks to house their wares. They set up huge carnival-style tents and then put out the fireworks on folding tables underneath the cover of the tents. I believe the rental company supplied both the tents and tables, but I didn't get to work on the tent. Imagine how many six-foot folding tables placed on their sides, stacked two-high, could be jammed into a Ryder truck with a thirty-foot cargo box. Well, the rental company knew how many tables were in there, and one other guy and I loaded and unloaded every one of them before lunch.[81]

The physical benefits of working hard certainly exceeded the monetary gain from working for $5 an hour. When I started the temp work, I was young, healthy, and fairly energetic. But I was not in work-shape. Work-shape is a far cry from gym shape. Gym-shape is about looking pretty and pumping iron in a completely

---

[81] Nowadays, if I tried to move even twenty tables, I would be off to my doctor to see if Lipitor is right for me. I'm joking. I'm a forty-year-old male; I never go to the doctor.

controlled, artificial environment. "Working out" serves no purpose except to enlarge or reduce the size of various parts of the body.[82] That's the whole objective. Work-shape isn't an objective at all. Work-shape is simply a by-product of having a real job to do. It has nothing to do with looking good or shaping the body because one's movements aren't controlled to isolate a specific muscle. So when I finally got into work-shape, I did not look like a bodybuilder. I probably didn't appear much different from when I started the grunt work. I could, however, feel the difference.

For my first temp job, I was sent to a construction site at the local mall.[83] When a new store moved into the mall, a general contractor was hired to transform the space to the store's specifications. In fact, some franchise stores would essentially have a store in a box (or I should say semi-trailer) with everything needed to make a Radio Shack, for instance. The contractor then hired whatever sub-contractors (electricians, plumbers, etc) were necessary to build the store. But sub-contractors don't unload supplies or clear debris, and that's where the temp guys came in. Anyway, on that first day after about four hours (it was just a ½ day job) of unloading and then emptying heavy cardboard boxes full of shelving, and then hoisting scrap metal and wood into a huge

---

[82] Some readers might point out that weightlifting and exercising prepare the body for athletic endeavors. This point is valid but not for 95% of the people who go to the gym.

[83] I was sent back to the mall several times during my short temp tenure.

dumpster, every muscle in my back and arms was thoroughly fatigued.[84] After only a few weeks of one strenuous job after another, I could tell that the heavy and often awkward lifting was getting easier. And I could see new temp guys, who apparently weren't working previously, struggling as I had earlier.

The hardest job I ever did as a temp worker was at the construction site of a new apartment complex on the western edge of town. Three of us were sent to help a concrete contractor pour gypsum concrete floors throughout the multi-level complex. The concrete mixer was stationed in the middle of the future parking lot of the complex. The mixed concrete was drawn from the mixer by a large, loud pump, which pumped the mix into a thick, long hose. Once the concrete started pumping, the hose was carried into every room on every level of the building, and just like that the apartment complex had uniform, smooth cement floors. We were informed right away that as soon as the machine started it would not (and could not) be stopped until the job was completed.[85]

The concrete contractor's crew consisted of three men: two to handle the hose and pour concrete and one to run the mixer. We

---

[84] If the reader has ever bought a large bookcase from IKEA, then he or she will have an idea of how heavy and awkward the cardboard boxes were.

[85] This information let us know that the temp agency's "rules" about mandatory breaks and lunchtime (which none of the employers adhered to anyway) would not apply to this particular job.

three temps all had the same job. We fed the mixer.[86] We shoveled sand into the mixer, or rather a bin above the actual mixer. And after a prescribed amount of sand was loaded into the bin, one of us lifted a ninety-pound bag of gypsum and dumped it in with the sand. While we all shoveled the whole time, we took turns on the cement bags. I should note that the full-time man assigned to the mixer also took a turn in the cement bag rotation. We shoveled and lifted non-stop (we couldn't even stop for a drink of water) for 5½ hours. When the job was completed, the mixer was shut down and the men who worked the hose began to clean and load their equipment. The contractor, whom we had seen in the morning before we started, did not return to sign our time cards.[87] The man who served as a de facto foreman signed our cards (he rounded our time up to an even six hours because we didn't get any breaks) and gave each of us a can of cold Coca-Cola.[88]

The cliché says if it doesn't kill you, it makes you stronger, and a few weeks later I was glad I had survived the cement mixer. I was sent out to the county fairgrounds on the north side of Springfield. My job, which wasn't supposed to take very long, consisted of helping put up tents (or canopies, really) for an

---

[86] I don't remember how water was added to the mix, but that wasn't part of our responsibilities.
[87] Apparently, the contractor spent his day bidding on and scheduling future jobs. Or maybe he played golf—I don't know.
[88] I normally drink diet soda, but I didn't have a problem with regular Coke at that moment.

upcoming car show at the fairgrounds. These tents needed to be anchored in the ground in case the unpredictable Springfield weather became unpredictable. So, as the tent guy and I put up each tent, we drove metal stakes into the ground and secured the tents with ropes. The problem for us, though, was that most of the tents needed to be set up on and around a large blacktop parking lot, which led us to quite a predicament. "How do you secure a tent on an asphalt surface?" I asked the tent guy.

After a short period of reflection, the tent guy decided that our only option was to pound the spikes through the pavement. I suppose I should have expressed some concern that the folks who ran the fairgrounds might not want their smooth parking lot dotted with holes that went down to the earth beneath the blacktop. Instead, I worried more about the effect that pounding metal spikes through asphalt with a sledgehammer might have on my back and arms. Call me selfish. Fortunately, as road surfaces go, blacktop is perhaps the softest and most pliable. I wouldn't want to try driving spikes into concrete. Of course, I didn't want to pound spikes into blacktop, either, but we did our John Henry act and the job got done without incident. And I have no idea what the fairgrounds people said or did when they saw those spike holes.

* * *

By and large, the men with whom I worked on these temp jobs were not much like me, except, of course, that we all needed the income, however meager, and we had few options. Some guys had lost jobs and had exhausted their unemployment. Some had recently come to town, hoping to find work associated with the Branson boom. Many of the guys hoped to catch on with one of the employers that used the temp workers.[89] And there were probably a few who were working only because their girlfriends or wives had threatened to kick them out if they didn't get some kind of a job. In short, they were down on their luck. But really, these men saw that for them earning a living meant a life of hard work, work that wasn't always safe and was rarely rewarding. I respected their resolve just to keep trying.

Some of these guys didn't have a lot going for them, and some were experiencing hard times, no doubt, because of bad choices (and maybe the reluctance to correct bad choices). One time I was sent out to a local beer distributor. Yes, I said "beer," which can lead a hard-working man to trouble. When I got to the beer distributor's facility, I discovered that two other temps and I had been called out to clean up a semi-trailer that had some trouble in transit. The trouble led to the senseless destruction of many, many cases of canned beer. The temps set about stacking, clearing,

---

[89] The temp agencies always use this hope of getting on full-time as a major lure for new temp workers.

sweeping, and dumping. After we had been working a while, the truck driver, who was more or less responsible for the mess, came to the back of the trailer and said, "I sure appreciate you boys workin' so hard and helpin' me out. Why dontchya'll set a couple uh cases off to the side for yer selves. They can't use none of this now." My fellow temps quickly put together two cases of scratched, but otherwise unharmed, cans and hid them out by the passenger side of the semi-trailer (away from the main building and office). Meanwhile, the truck driver kept talking, "I never hauled any alcohol before. Man, what hard asses! You got to be inspected practically everywhere."

It never dawned on the truck driver or my fellow temps that such a heavily regulated industry might require the beer people to account for every beer. But when we were about finished with the job, the beer people looked everything over and said, "There are two cases (out of hundreds) missing. Where are they?" No one, including me, said anything. "Well," the head beer man said, "nobody leaves or gets paid until we get those cases." Again, no one said anything, and the beer guys went about some other important beer business. After a few minutes of worried silence among the temp crew and truck driver, I walked around the front of the truck, picked up the cases, walked back to the end of the trailer, and set them down next to a stack of damaged cases. I never said a word to anyone, and no one said anything to me, including the beer people. We got our timecards signed, and the truck driver finally said, "Sorry about that fellas." [90]

In my fellow workers' defense, I have to say that the beer guys were mostly jerks. The back of that trailer was a stinky mess, and to get the count they needed they had to count can fragments and smashed cans. And they could have explained to a bunch of flunkies like us that they needed to account for every last beer. What made this incident humorous to me is that inside the beer warehouse, the company had vending machines in the workers' break room. These machines were not full of soda or junk food. They sold their own beer in vending machines to their own employees who were on the job. And they sold the beer for about 50 cents a can. So an employee could have a beer at morning break, lunch, and afternoon break. At least my fellow temps would have waited to drink their "stolen" beer until after they were off the clock.

* * *

---

[90] One beer employee was paid to push a broom around the warehouse all day. This long-legged young man was maybe 6'4" or 6'5" and wore athletic clothing (sneakers, shorts, etc). Though he was not what you might call bulked up, he looked big, lean, and strong—like a guy who could throw a ninety-five mile per hour fastball, or hit one. And although the other employees exchanged pleasantries with him, no one ever seemed to give him directions or an order. He was too old to be a current college athlete getting paid a high wage to do nothing, so my best guess was that he worked at the distributorship so he could do his real job of playing for a company-sponsored softball team. I had seen it before. Back in California, I knew of top players who "worked" for dairies and construction companies and so on.

All of these odd-job adventures took place between January and August of 1993. In August, I received my PhD, and we moved back to California. I remained under-employed for the better part of two more years, so the desperate need for income and the willingness to do just about anything for a buck didn't evaporate when Southern Illinois University conferred its Doctor of Philosophy degree upon me. But I never worked for a temp agency again. Every day, I see the kind of guys who worked with me for the temp agency, guys with tattoos and poor English skills. When I was a workin' man, I tried not to let on who or what I am. It was too hard to explain, and it didn't matter as long as I could do the work as well as the next man. Now as I sit and eat my breakfast at Jack-in-the-Box, writing in a notebook made in China (how can that be?) about my old adventures, I watch these coarse men in their work clothes get their breakfast and ready themselves for the hard and perhaps dirty work they must do today. They look strong and weary, and they don't pay any attention to me.

Coming Home?

Until I met my wife, I had never been anyone's first choice. I was a second son, second-team all-conference in high school (football and baseball), and I attended what one might call second-tier schools. I didn't get into Stanford or UC Berkeley or the Ivy League schools as an undergraduate, and those schools were just as uninterested in me when I applied for graduate school.[91] So it should not have surprised me when, as I finished my PhD and applied for jobs, the employment offers failed to overwhelm me. Still, I had always managed to achieve a modest level of success, and I was more than a little disappointed that I

---

[91] Let me say here that I have never been disappointed with the education I received at CSU, Stanislaus and SIUC.

couldn't even get an interview. I had done my graduate work diligently and in a timely fashion, and I had attempted to do the extra but necessary things (getting articles published, reading papers at conferences) to make myself "hirable." I understood, too, that there were larger economical and political reasons for a tight job market, which only encouraged me to feel helpless and hopeless.

Hope did come, though, midway through the spring of 1993. I had previously applied for the same job Paula had at Southwest Missouri. Each year, their English Department hired a handful of full-time instructors who were then given a five-year term of employment. When the five years were up, the instructor moved on. I would have preferred a permanent, tenure-track position somewhere, but we figured that if I got a job at Southwest, we would be secure for at least four years—when Paula's term would expire. One day, we got a call from the English Department secretary. She asked me to bring in all my supporting employment documents (transcripts, recommendation letters, etc.) immediately because the hiring committee wanted the complete files of the finalists for the jobs. When we delivered all the information to the department, we were given every indication that an interview (and most likely employment) was imminent. And then, even though Paula was a member of their department, we never heard officially from them again, not even a form rejection letter.

For that brief period of time when we thought I would be hired by SMS, we allowed ourselves to think about putting down roots (at least for awhile) in Springfield. We looked at houses for sale, we made friends, and, most importantly but not entirely because of the hope of a job, we started a family. We found out Paula was pregnant early that summer, and thus the need and hope for a job reached a higher level of urgency. But nothing ever happened. As the date of my graduation approached, the pressure to decide what to do with ourselves increased. Frankly, Paula was a bit outraged that SMS had not even interviewed me after saying I was a top candidate, so she was of the opinion that she should quit her job and we should move home to California—where family could help us and friends at local colleges might hire us.

Even though I agreed with this plan, I could never have suggested we take such a course of action. It was not my place to tell Paula to give up a real job that she had earned. She could have easily and rightfully said that we should stay in Springfield, where she could work and bring in some income while I would continue the job search and maybe work part-time. Instead, I think the beautiful baby in her tummy was telling her it was time to go home. Thus, Paula officially informed the SMS Department of English that they could kindly kiss her sweet asseola (which it is), and she resigned from her position as English instructor.

* * *

The rest of this story shows what can happen when two intelligent, educated but desperate people make one bad decision. The bad decision was not the one to move home to California. No, the misguided idea was how we planned to make the move. Get this: we invited our mothers (one newly re-married, the other newly divorced) to fly back for my gradation, help us load our stuff in a rental truck, and then drive home with us. You have to understand our predicament. We were broke (of course), and Paula was great with morning sickness.[92] So it made sense to get help from home, since there was none readily available in Springfield. Paula's mom, of course, wanted to see her now that Paula was pregnant, and my mom thought she should be there for my graduation.

At SIU, commencement exercises are held in December (at the end of the fall term) and August (for summer term), as well as the traditional springtime date. Summer is the smallest graduation ceremony of the three. For the other two, the university holds several different ceremonies across campus for the various colleges within the university, but for summer everyone is together, across disciplines and degree programs. The key part of the PhD

---

[92] Paula's experience with morning sickness went like this: she said, "You know, I was reading about morning sickness in a book, and it said that less than 20% of all mothers really get morning sickness. And I'm not one to get sick easily. So, I think there's a good chance that I won't even get morning...BARF!"

graduation ceremony is receiving one's doctoral hood, which becomes an integral part of the academic regalia. Doctoral candidates at SIU are "hooded" by their dissertation advisor, so my advisor, Dr. A-J Morey, graciously attended the ceremony with me and put the hood over me on the SIU Arena stage. Afterwards, she joined us for lunch at a local Chinese restaurant. Talk about worlds colliding: mother, mother-in-law, wife, and dissertation director. Luckily, A-J had a little daughter at home, and that (what with Paula expecting) gave us something about which to talk.

During lunch, A-J and I exchanged gifts. She gave me a copy of her new scholarly book (which I had requested), and I gave her a cheaply bound copy of the dissertation she had just directed. Those gifts were then passed around the table. A-J's book was about religion and sexuality in 19th century American literature, so it went through the mothers' hands like a hot potato. I remember, though, that my mom held my dissertation (what the day was all about, really), looked at the cover and presumably the title for several seconds, nodded at it convincingly, brushed it with the back of her hand, and set it down on the table between the plates of tasty Chinese food.

After lunch, we drove back to the university to take some pictures. Four years, almost to the day, after we pulled into Carbondale (and I thought the heat and humidity would kill me), we stood in our best clothes (Paula in a beautiful white maternity dress, me with my hair matted down from the mortar board), smiling at the camera, enjoying the lovely campus for the last time. Then we drove "home" to Springfield to prepare for the voyage "home." We have not been back to Carbondale since that day in 1993.[93] For the trip home, we had rented a too-big Ryder truck. Four years earlier, we had used a Budget truck and towed our Dodge Colt on a tow dolly. This time, we sold the Colt to pay for the Ryder truck. There would be no tow dolly for the trip home. Paula, her mother, and my mother would drive home in our Ford Tempo. I, on the other hand, would lead the caravan west in the Ryder truck, with Olivia the beagle riding shotgun and serving as my sidekick/navigator/co-pilot.[94] Occasionally, one of the women would join Livy and me in the truck, but it really bothered the dog. Poor pregnant Paula had to drive almost the whole way in the Tempo. The mothers talked so much that Paula figured the one person paying attention to the road should do the driving.

The trip from Springfield to Modesto, California is about 1,800 miles. When Paula and I made trips across county during our stay in the Midwest, we found that we could do about 600 miles a day, fairly comfortably. And we figured out that we could do 600

---

[93] From time to time, we get fundraising calls from the university (students, actually, calling for the Alumni Association, the English Department, the general fund). They always ask if we have been back to SIUC "to see all the changes." Usually, though, when the student fundraiser sees that we live in California, the conversation shifts to what California is really like.

[94] It's good to be the man. Sometimes.

miles in about 10 hours, including pit stops. That means for our final trip home, we should have been able to make it home in about three days, with two nights at motels. However, this trek was not the typical trip home. We had four adults (one pregnant), two vehicles (one with its top speed limited to 62 mph), and a hound dog. To be fair, the dog added no time to the trip. And we made the decision before we left that this would be the one time we stopped and took the side trip to the Grand Canyon. We could not grow old knowing that we had driven through Arizona four or five times and never once gone to the Grand Canyon.

The first leg of the journey went well enough. We drove from Springfield to Amarillo, Texas, where the weather was miserably hot and I noticed the Ryder truck was beginning to run a little warm. Before we left Amarillo the next morning, Paula tried to secure a motel room for the night in the Williams-Flagstaff area.[95] It was at this point that we discovered that our timing was just a bit off. Apparently, some guy named the Pope was visiting the southwest and holding a youth festival. There were very few hotel rooms available in the state of Arizona. At every stop during our journey out of Texas and through New Mexico, Paula tried to find

---

[95] In those days, kids, to make a call on the road you had to stop and find a pay phone. A few people had cell phones, but not us. I remember the first mobile phone I ever used came with its own suitcase. That was in 1989 just before we got married. I was driving the "service wagon" at the Mercedes dealership where my dad worked, and they had just put the phone in the car, and it took up the whole passenger seat.

us a room. We were forced to settle for a Super 8 in Holbrook, Arizona—well east of our desired goal for the day. We stopped early enough in the day for us to go down to the motel's pool. Paula's mom elected to stay in the room and freshen up. A few seconds after we got to the pool, my mom began talking to the other guests who were sitting poolside. These other guests ("small world!") were also from Modesto. As we sat by the pool, we watched the sun begin to set and a thunderstorm begin to develop far on the desert horizon. The storm organized quickly and moved toward the hotel. We were soon engulfed in rain, lightning, and thunder. There may have even been hail; I'm not sure. We took cover near the pool and waited out the storm. Unfortunately, before the storm passed over, it knocked out the power at the motel.

When the power went out we figured we should go back to the room before the day turned completely dark. Frankly, we had not given much thought to Paula's mom being back in the room during the storm. However, upon our return to the room, we discovered that Paula's mom, Lynda, had just entered the shower when the lights went off. As one might expect in a basic motel room, absolutely no natural light shown into the bathroom. So, as the old joke goes, when the light went out, she was really in the dark—in the shower, in the bathroom, in a cheap motel, in the desert, alone. I believe she felt a little better when we finally returned to the room, though I'm sure for a few long moments she thought she was in a Hitchcock movie. In the waning light after the storm, the motel guests loitered about just outside their rooms, talking to their neighbors for the night, hoping that the power would be restored before we tried to sleep through the hot Arizona night. However, we had no choice but retreat into the darkness of our room and sleep without the aid of the air conditioner.

The next day we felt the impact of being forced to stop before we wanted. Instead of getting up in Williams and driving in the car to the Grand Canyon, we were forced to travel from Holbrook to Williams. We had to find a safe parking place for the rental truck and then head for the canyon. When we arrived in Williams, we cleared some stuff, including my mother's suitcase, out of the car to make room for the dog and me. The drive to the south rim of the canyon took us the better part of an hour. When we got there, we stopped, found a parking place, and then walked to one of the vista points. Sure enough, as we approached the rim we discovered that the canyon is one big-ass hole in the ground. I also realized that the Grand Canyon offers visitors only two options: (1) serious exploration requiring time and exertion and (2) a cursory survey of the vista. We opted for the latter Grand Canyon experience.

Luckily, we had a video recorder along with us, and I planned to use the camcorder to preserve our visit for posterity. The camcorder, which was an early model made by a now-defunct TV brand called Curtis Mathes, belonged to my father, who had loaned the camera to my mother, his ex-wife, so that she could videotape my graduation ceremony.[96] Unfortunately, my mother was incapable of operating the machine, and she foisted it upon Paula, who was trying to watch me graduate. The footage we got was slightly worse than the quality of the Zapruder film. After the ceremony, the camera was tucked away into the corner of the Tempo's trunk for the ride to California. As we stood at the precipice of the great gap in the earth, I turned to my mom and asked, "Would you mind getting the camcorder our of the car? I'll take some footage, and then we can get back on the road."

Mom said, "But it's not in the car."

"What do you mean?" I asked. "It's been in the car for a thousand miles."

"I thought I had better put it in my suitcase for safe keeping. And you put my suitcase in the back of the truck." If not for the presence of my wife and unborn child, one less person might have returned to the Tempo for the ride back to Williams. I just said, "Okay then. We're done."

We pressed on through the afternoon and into the early evening. When we drove into the oasis of Needles, California the temperature had gone down to a balmy 112 degrees Fahrenheit—

---

[96] Apparently, the divorce agreement left him with the camcorder and her with the Curtis Mathes VCR, which remained functional until 2004.

down from the day's high of 117 degrees. At that point, the truck's cooling system decided it needed a break and the temperature gauge pushed into the danger range.[97] Fortunately, Ryder had an 800 number we could call for service on the rental truck. But we would have to spend the night in Needles because it would take a considerable amount of time to get someone to check out the truck.[98] While the ladies in our party settled into our room and then ventured out to the pool (which featured misters built into the poolside patio), I sat out by the truck, waiting the mechanic's arrival. When the mechanic found me, he checked the cooling system on the truck. As far as he could tell, the only real problem we had was that the truck was quite low on coolant—which I should have taken car of myself, but you pay for the roadside assistance when you rent the truck. By the time the mechanic diagnosed the problem, it was late enough for all the stores nearby to be closed. He had to return to his shop to rustle up some coolant. So I sat by the truck again until he returned.

In checking out the truck and its paperwork, the mechanic and I discovered that the truck was due for its 30,000-mile service, but the service had not yet been completed. You see, when I picked up the truck from the rental outfit in Springfield, the truck had

---

[97] Attentive readers will remember from "Santa Rosa, 6:00 AM" that when Paula and I moved east in the Budget rental truck we drove in the cool of the night. Those same readers will also realize that if we didn't stop now in Needles, the overheating truck would have to make it 200 miles to Barstow.

[98] In all our travels between California and Illinois, then Missouri, Paula and I had never needed to spend the night in California.

something like 29,500 miles on it. Instead of performing the service, the boys in Springfield, knowing the truck was heading one way to California, elected to leave the service for the next rental store—because, after all, the truck didn't have 30,000 miles on it when it left Springfield. But I'm not bitter. I mean, it was quite pleasant out there in the motel parking lot. By midnight, the temperature had dropped into the 90s. The mechanic wished me luck and suggested we get an early start in the morning—before it got hot in Needles. I went up to the motel room and set the alarm for 4:00 am.

With 600 miles to go, we were on the road well before six, and the sunrise chased us into Barstow. The truck's temperature stayed under control the rest of the way home, but I didn't allow myself the luxury of the air-conditioner until we were safely in the great Central Valley—where we knew if the Ryder failed us, our family would come to the rescue.

The Honking Lady: A Brief Tale of Woe and a Bundle of Joy

I magine the pride I felt, as a young man with a PhD, to move my pregnant wife into the same old duplex in Turlock she shared with her sister before we got married. Various members of Paula's family had inhabited this ancient rental over the course of several years. First, Paula's brother-in-law, Dave, before he was her brother-in-law, lived in the duplex on Syracuse Avenue with friends while he attended CSU, Stanislaus. Then, when Dave married Paula's sister, Gena, they lived there briefly. Later, Paula's younger sister Tracy lived there with a roommate. And shortly after Paula and I met, she moved in the duplex with Tracy. Finally, in 1993, as Paula and I prepared to move back to California, we discovered that the Syracuse duplex was available. The rent was lower than anything else on the west coast, and we decided that living there beat moving in with family.

Our side of the duplex was really a charming little dump. We had the use of a small garage, which was really about the size of a shed, and there was a very small backyard where the dog could do her business. Directly behind the duplex stood Turlock's most notoriously bad apartment complex. Over at the apartment complex, a terrible property owner and worse tenants combined to create a den of drugs, violence, and unsafe living conditions. But other than the noise (loud music, police sirens, fire crackers, yelling, etc.), we never actually had any trouble from the apartment people.

Our new neighbors on the other side of the duplex were a young Mexican couple. They were also expecting a baby—about the same time Paula was due. And at that time, the wife's brother was living with them in the duplex. The wife, whose name I don't remember, didn't come out of the house very often. The husband, Mario, was a gregarious fellow who worked as a manager of a locally owned Mexican restaurant, which, of course, meant he worked a long day. He left the duplex mid to late morning to open for lunch and came home late at night, well after the restaurant closed at 10:00 pm. He worked at least six nights a week. His late night return became a routine for all of us living in the rental property. When he came home, Mario's wife was apparently always fast asleep. And apparently the door was always locked and could only be opened from the inside. So, Mario pounded (I mean pounded) on the door. Now, due to the odd layout (I hesitate to call it a "floor plan") of the old duplex, when he pounded on his door, it sounded like he was pounding on our bedroom wall.

When the pounding failed to rouse his bride, Mario had no choice (apparently) but to begin hollering. "Mario! Mario! Es su esposo!" he yelled two, maybe three times, with a little more pounding.[99] Once he was granted access to his home, Mario began doing the chores his pregnant wife was unable to do during the day, which means he fired up the vacuum cleaner. You know, when you live in a thin-walled old duplex and the neighbor does his or her vacuuming in the middle of the day, when the world is alive and noisy, you don't really notice the vacuuming at all. However, after midnight the neighbor's vacuum sounds like a 747 preparing for takeoff. Mario's homecomings really did become a nightly routine for us. We would go to sleep for an hour or two, and then Mario would come home and we would be up for about an hour. Then, when their apartment was nice and tidy, we all tried to go back to sleep.

I mentioned before that Mario's brother-in-law was living with Mario and his wife when we moved in to the duplex.

---

[99] We were never sure why Mario yelled his own name. We thought maybe she was saying, "Who is it?" when he pounded on the door.

Tragically, Mario's wife didn't approve of her brother's girlfriend. In fact, Mario's wife would not allow the girlfriend to enter the duplex. The ban, however, did not deter the girlfriend from visiting the brother frequently. She simply drove her Chrysler Lebaron convertible up to the house, parked at the curb, and honked. I should say, rather, that she honked until the brother came out of the house and joined her in the car. Occasionally, they would drive off together and come back some time later. These visits, I suppose, we would call dates. More often, though, when the brother got into the car with his girlfriend, they would just sit there in the car—sometimes making out, sometimes simply talking. For some reason, I think the brother's name was Noe, but I could not tell you the name of his girlfriend. We just called her the Honking Lady.

* * *

As soon as we moved into the Syracuse duplex, Paula and I commenced a desperate job search. Paula quickly found temporary employment (an office job) through a friend. Because I had earned a teaching credential before I completed my MA at CSU, Stanislaus, I thought I would apply for secondary teaching jobs, as long as nothing was happening on the college front. The initial term of my credential was about to expire, so I called the Stanislaus County Office of Education to inquire about an extension. I told the woman on the phone that I had been going to graduate school and teaching out of state for the last four years and wanted to get my credential renewed. She said, "In order to get your Clear Credential renewed for another five years, you need to have completed the required 'Professional Development.'"

"I just finished my PhD."

"You need to do enough hours of development in your field."

"I just finished a PhD <u>in English</u>. I have been teaching college English for four years."

"Well, you need a mentor teacher to help you plan your professional development. Normally, teachers take extension hours or education units."

"Did I mention I earned a Master's degree and a doctorate since I was awarded the credential?" I found myself in a hopeless battle to allow me to do work I didn't really want to do. Eventually, though, I was granted a temporary, emergency extension to my credential so I could look for work.

I landed a few interviews but no offers. In one interview, the vice-principal of a junior high school picked a verbal fight with me over 1) the requirements of my degree versus his, and 2) the use of grammar exercises in the teaching of writing. I also applied for non-teaching jobs, but I didn't have much of a chance. What could I say when the manager of a sporting goods store asked, "What do you see yourself doing in five years?" Some might call it pride, but I couldn't honestly say I hoped to be selling hunting and fishing licenses. One of my non-teaching applications, though, led to my first ray of hope. I had put the name of one of my former professors down as a reference on an application. The company, a cheese distributor, never called me for an interview, but they called my references. When my professor and friend John Carroll got the cheese company's call, he told the department chair that they should try to give me some work. A few weeks later, I was asked to take over a class at the last minute. At about the same time, I got a job teaching three or four hours a day at a private school for dyslexic children. This job at the dyslexic school was not ultimately a good experience (I lasted there for about three months), but with my two jobs and Paula's job we were bringing in enough to make the minimum payments on the credit cards.

By the time our baby was born in late January 1994, I was teaching two classes at CSU, Stanislaus and two at Modesto Junior College. Paula gave birth to Emily and immediately began teaching a class at CSUS as well. Paula woke up in labor on the morning of January 28. We went to the hospital in Modesto, and just like that, at 2:12 a.m., on January 29, we had our precious Emily. It was just your typical twenty-one hour labor. Amazingly, our nurse-midwife, a nice woman named Irene, stayed with us for most of those twenty-one hours.[100] The long labor was more agonizing, perhaps, because we had chosen not to learn the sex of the baby before the birth. Despite the practical advantages of knowing whether it's a boy or girl beforehand, Paula and I felt that the baby's sex was meant to be a surprise. And it's the responsibility (and joy) of the parents-to-be to select one male name and one female name prior to the baby's birth. Our names were Elijah and Emily. Because both names start with the letter "E," we took to calling the baby in Paula's belly "Tiny E"—from a *Saturday Night Live* sketch with Nicolas Cage called "Tiny Elvis."

So after nine months and twenty-one hours we were dying to know if we had an Elijah or an Emily. When the baby finally made her appearance and Paula looked to me, I cried out, "It's an Emily!"[101] Mommy and baby were healthy and safe, and we were finally able to say "Goodnight, Irene" to our midwife as the nurses moved us to a room in the maternity ward.

The next morning, Paula was recovering fairly well, though Emily was already showing us that she was not going to be one of those sleepy babies. At some point, Paula finished feeding the baby, put her down, hoping she would sleep, and then she went into the

---

[100] For those of you kids out there thinking about procreating, I have some advice: have a nurse-midwife handle the delivery. Two years after Emily was born, Irene's colleague, a midwife named Carolyn, delivered our second daughter Abigail. Irene and Carolyn gave Paula and our babies the best care possible.

[101] Emily still loves to hear mom or dad talk about how we had an "Emily." Emily, by the way, was not a popular name in 1994. It then became the number one baby name for at least ten years.

bathroom in the hospital room. I was sitting in a chair next to our baby, dozing, when I looked up and saw my dad and my grandmother (his mother). I had only seen my dad a few times since he had moved in with his girlfriend and her sons, and I had not seen my grandmother in maybe six years.[102] This book isn't about old Schmidt family gripes, grievances, and grudges, but I should note that I do not think my dad had seen my grandmother in those six years, either. If the reader is wondering, the answer is, no, my grandmother did not attend our wedding, but she was certainly invited. I give the reader all this buildup so that you can begin to picture in your reading mind the look on Paula's face when she shuffled out of the bathroom and saw first my dad and then our baby in the arms of my grandmother, whom she had never met (she quickly figured out that this was the old lady who had ignored her husband's birthdays when he was a child).

Because this was my first trip to the Twilight Zone, I don't remember much of what was said or what happened. I recall that Paula said, "Hi, Ernie" to my dad, and I said, "Polly, this is my Grandma, Emma." Polly took Emily from her, and I'm sorry but I seem to have blocked out anything else.[103]

---

[102] Things have been better with my father for many years. He has lived in the Seattle area for quite a while now, but the kids get a big kick out of their grandpa when they get to see him.

[103] Ironically, Yours Truly is now the person responsible for paying Grandma's bills and doing her business. She's in her late-eighties and living in a nursing home.

We made the mistake of bringing our baby home on Super Bowl Sunday. Somehow, we ended up with an impromptu combination Welcome Home Baby/Super Bowl party in the tiny living room of the Syracuse duplex. I bet there were a dozen or more family members sitting around, eating pizza, watching the game, and meeting Emily. Paula was set up in the bedroom and periodically an envoy from the living room went in to check on her and the baby. The next day we realized that perhaps Paula and I had overestimated the progress of her recovery, and maybe I should not have invited people to stay and watch the game.

* * *

Within a week of Emily's birth, our duplex neighbors' baby was born. I caught up with Mario one morning as he was on his way to the restaurant. I asked about the baby. He was thrilled to have a son.

"Did your wife have a long labor?" I asked.

"Yeah, it took her a while, like three or four hours."

"Oh really. Did you guys do the Lamaze classes?"

"The what?"

"The child birth class at the hospital. You know, the breathing lessons and all that."

"Oh. No, she didn't do nothing like that. She just went in and had it."

"Well, I'm very happy for you."

"Thank you. Congratulations to you, too."

I waited several weeks before I told Paula about my conversation with Mario. A few months later, we moved out of the Syracuse duplex. I was able to teach summer classes at MJC and CSUS, and we somehow managed to rent a neat little old house on Park Street in Turlock, where we would live until we bought our home in Modesto in 1996.

One Rider's Beginnings

Part 1: Forgive me, Ms. Welty

You know you are a rider if you have had more bikes (dirt bikes, ATVs) than women. My first motorcycle was a 1978 Kawasaki KE 175. The bike was slightly used when I bought it in the fall of 1993. I do not count the mini-bike my brother and I briefly rode as kids. We briefly rode it because it briefly ran. The one time I really remember riding the mini-bike, I wrecked it when I tried to jump over a big hump in the middle of a logging road. I got literally inches of air before the mini-bike's lack of suspension encouraged me to fly over the handlebars. I also do not count the old Puch moped that we bought for $50 from Paula's Uncle Bob just before we moved to Illinois in 1989. The Puch and I soon developed a very close relationship, as it served as my primary mode of transportation throughout my first year in graduate school. I rode the Puch all over campus and the town of Carbondale, often at speeds in excess of 25 mph.

As the reader probably knows, the moped is designed to be a sort of motorcycle-bicycle hybrid. Supposedly, one can use it as either a motorcycle (a scooter, really) or a bicycle, but believe me when I say that the moped makes for a piss-poor bicycle—unless, of course, you would like to provoke a heart attack. Basically, though, a moped works like this: the rider turns on the key, sets the choke (if necessary), pedals the bicycle pedals like crazy, and then twists the throttle with his/her right hand on the handlebar. The small two-stroke engine ignites, and the moped can then move under its own power. The rider can elect to supplement the engine's ability to power the bike by continuing to pedal, or he/she can simply ride along with his or her feet resting on the pedals. If the engine fails to start, which is almost always the case, the entire process must be repeated. There is no kick-starter or electric start.

The pedal-start system works okay when the ambient temperature is higher than 70 degrees Fahrenheit. You see, pedaling with the key on and the choke on essentially warms up the engine so it can be started and run. But when it is cold outside, pedaling can't warm the engine enough, so it dies immediately—if it ignites at all. The engine won't start unless the throttle is engaged, but the choke goes off as soon as the throttle goes on, and the engine won't fire if the bike's not moving. What I'm trying to say is that if the rider could keep the choke on, the engine could run and warm up without the bike moving. In short, it could sit and idle. But the transmission won't allow that to happen. With the moped it was all (which wasn't much) or nothing.

For my first semester of teaching at SIU, I was assigned two Freshman Composition courses that were scheduled back-to-back at 8:00 am and 9:00 am. The first class ended at 8:50, so I had ten minutes to wrap up one class and get to the next. And I was done teaching by 10:00 am. It was a great schedule, except that the second class was located about a ten-minute walk from the first one. Enter the Puch. I was able to park very close to the first class in a motorcycle parking area in a parking garage. At the conclusion of the first class, I gathered everything into a backpack, hustled to the parking garage, put my stuff in an old milk crate I had attached to the back of the Puch, exited the garage, drove out the driveway, crossed over US 51 into the parking lot for the other building (which was actually a high-rise student dormitory), and hurried into the first-floor makeshift classroom.

The moped as primary transportation worked fine until the weather turned cold. I bought a huge simulated down parka that was on sale at Sears. It was reversible and weatherproof, and it came with a nifty hood that could cover most of my head and face (no easy task). If only the parka could warm up the moped the way it warmed me. The Puch had to sit outside at night in the motorcycle area of our Evergreen Terrace parking lot. I had to start the moped on many, many below freezing mornings. And as it got colder, the farther I had to pedal to get it started and keep it running. So it would be say twenty degrees outside at 7:15 am, and I would hop on the moped, wearing my big coat, and I would start pedaling.[104] I pedaled out the entrance of our parking lot and hit the throttle. No start. I pedaled down the main driveway of the apartment complex and hit the throttle. No start. I pedaled across Pleasant Hill Road and hit the throttle. By that point it often started. Inside my parka I was a ball of sweat and a little lighted headed. As the moped picked up speed, the icy wind chilled my overheated body and I slumped over on the Puch and waited for my body to recover from my morning exercise. Most mornings, Paula watched the whole agonizing process from our apartment's tiny balcony. On the moped I could not hear her laughter, but sometimes she took pictures.

* * *

---

[104] You must visualize my stuff in the milk crate behind me bouncing side to side as I pedaled furiously, my butt up off the seat, my head leaning forward, and my mouth cursing.

No person is more responsible for me becoming a rider than Paula. Not long after I met her, Paula told me about her family's property in the mountains (which the family calls either "the property" or "the mountains"), where many branches of the clan gather to ride dirtbikes.[105] My first visit to the property came during Thanksgiving weekend of 1988. Because of my lack of riding experience and skill, I was forced to ride as a passenger behind Paula on her Honda Trail 90.[106] It did not take long for her to try to climb a small embankment and flip me off the back of the bike. But she couldn't get rid of me that easily. I was already hooked. The old trailers, the remote location, the hidden trails, the challenge of riding and staying upright—it all kind of spoke to me. It said, "This is your destiny, young man." Well, that's a little corny. But I was in love—with Paula.[107]

---

[105] At that time (1988), nobody had any ATVs, though there were a few old gas-powered golf carts that were used to haul people up and down trails. The golf carts were actually made by Harley-Davidson during the era when AMF owned Harley. They were powered by 250cc engines, and one was a three-wheeler with an oblong center-mounted steering wheel-bar. We actually tried to rebuild one of the golf carts after the kids were born. But after a small investment and considerable work, the effort was abandoned, as was the cart.

[106] The Honda 90, which has not been manufactured for many years, remains a hot commodity on the used market. It's a popular choice of RV owners, who carry the bikes along for riding around the campground or running to the store. The little bike's popularity, though, in no way diminishes the fact that it is a worthless deathtrap—or it would be if it had any power. Its tires are too small and skinny; its weight is unbalanced; its center of gravity is too high; and it's just plain ugly.

[107] In fact, we first talked of marriage that weekend in the mountains.

Actually, I had grown up traveling through the backcountry and camping, but my dad was a jeeper, not a rider. He was introduced to off-roading by his friend and fellow mechanic J.B. Scott (if you are wondering what the J.B. stood for, the answer is nothing. His name was "J.B."). We belonged to a jeep club, and Dad even raced 4X4s in sand drags, hill climbs, and cross-country events for several years. The biggest difference between "wheeling" (when I was a kid we called it jeeping) and riding is that wheeling only requires one person to do the work, unless you encounter terrain rough enough for someone to get out of the vehicle and act as a spotter. When you ride motorcycles or quads, everyone is involved. Each rider must negotiate his/her way down the trail. Admittedly, when we ride we must make sure the difficulty of the trail doesn't overmatch the skills of the riders in the group. And Aunt Betty might not be able to come along if she can't do her own riding.[108]

The four years we were in Illinois and Missouri slowed the progress of my riding (if we don't count the moped), although we came close to purchasing a motorcycle on more than one occasion. We went to the property when we were home for breaks, but any riding I did was on borrowed equipment. When we came home to

---

[108] Several ATV companies have addressed the Aunt Betty problem with new motorized products. We now have two-person side-by-side utility vehicles that drive almost like mini-jeeps and also two-rider ATVs, which allow enthusiasts to do legally what we have sometimes done illegally on conventional ATVs. And there is no Aunt Betty.

California for good, Paula suggested that I take my graduation money and buy a motorcycle. Even though we had other, more important, "needs" for which the money could be used, I concurred that I should find a bike as soon as possible. I bought my Kawasaki from a guy who lived in an apartment complex in Oakdale, California. I took along my brother-in-law Ritch to check it out (he had a Toyota pickup to haul it home). Ritch was as mechanically inept as I was, but we examined the Kawasaki as thoroughly as we could. We started it, rode it, checked the clutch and gears, etc., and then I paid $325 for it. Fortunately, when the family got a look at the bike, it passed the Uncle Bob and Uncle Warren test. Neither uncle thought I had been ripped off.[109]

As I said at the beginning of this piece, the old Kawasaki was a KE 175, which meant that it was powered by a 175cc two-stroke engine that produced an incredible sixteen horsepower when it left the factory. As far as I know the "E" in KE stood for "enduro," a term common in cross-country and endurance racing, that in this case signified that the dirtbike was street legal.[110] It was a good thing I could ride the Kawasaki on the street because we

---

[109] It's amazing what a difference thirteen years and a steady job can make. Today, I don't think I would even look at a fifteen-year-old bike, unless it was some kind of collector's item.

[110] Today, a dirtbike that is also legal for street use is referred to as a "dual-sport" motorcycle. Each of the major manufacturers (Honda, Suzuki, Yamaha, Kawasaki) makes one or two of these models, but they aren't as common as they were in the seventies. Here I will make a criminal confession: at the time I rode the Kawi on the street I did not have motorcycle license.

were down to one car at the time. During the fall of 1993, I rode the bike all around Turlock. I rode it to CSU, Stanislaus to teach my one class there and then over to the school for dyslexic children, where I taught in the afternoon.

At the property, the Kawasaki went pretty well everywhere I wanted to go. Back then, just about everybody on our side of the family rode old enduro-type machines. In fact, when we went out for a long ride, we expected somebody to break down. We carried tools, spark plugs, and towropes. So my Kawasaki fit right in with the rest. Actually, it ran better than some for maybe two years. The Kawi's highlight came one Thanksgiving weekend when we woke up on Friday morning to find several inches of snow surrounding the trailers. We went for a beautiful ride that morning. When we came to Schoolhouse Ridge, I decided to have a go at it in the snow—and the little green machine chugged and slipped and dug down and made it all the way to the top. I whooped and hollered the whole way.

Eventually, I started having trouble with the carburetor and we also had to fiddle with the exhaust. It ran off and on for a while longer, until we figured out that the CDI ignition was the real problem. That's when I lost hope in the old Kawi. An ignition box might seem like a minor ailment to cause the retirement of a bike. However, replacing the ignition would cost more than I had paid for the whole bike.

As the Kawasaki went into decline, I began to borrow more and more the Yamaha TT 500 that belonged to Paula's Uncle Bob. The old TT 500 was a big four-stroke, or "thumper," and it was the fastest bike I had ever ridden. It was heavy. And even though the suspension was probably state of the art for 1977, the TT was a bit of a beast until you got it going at a decent speed. But it was a blast to ride, and those riders in the family who could handle it earned the right to brag a little about their exploits on it. I am still grateful to Uncle Bob for allowing me to take my turn on the TT. He was always very gracious and generous: "You can ride the TT any time you like," he said. "Just make sure that when you fall you get yourself between the bike and the ground."

While few riders rode the TT, even fewer could actually start it. The big bike had a kick-starter that could break your ankle and/or foot if you didn't do it correctly. There was just too much compression in that engine for a rider just to hop on and start kicking. So Yamaha devised a compression release starting system that worked like this: at the top of the engine case there was a glass window or bubble. Inside this bubble there was a silver tab that rotated in and out of view with the revolutions of the engine. When the tab was visible and perfectly aligned in the bubble, the kick-starter could be kicked without severe injury to the kicker. To get the silver tab into the position, the rider pulled the compression release lever, located on the left side of the handlebars along with the clutch lever, and then worked the kick-starter while watching for the tab. Of course, even after you did all this, there was no guarantee it would actually start.

The best way to start the TT was to push or roll start it. You could put it in gear, pull in the compression release, and roll down a hill and be reasonably assured that it would fire up. On starting the TT, Uncle Bob always offered us the following bit of wisdom: "Remember, gravity is your friend if you're trying to start the TT. So make sure you always park the damn thing on a hill." This was sage advice indeed, and I can remember parking the TT fifty yards away from everyone else when we took a break on a long ride—just so I'd be able to roll it down a hill when it was time to leave.[111]

Part 2: Where I Rode; What I Rode For

Later in the nineties, all-terrain vehicles (ATVs) began to show up among the family's rolling stock. The three-wheelers of the 1980s had never really caught on with us, but quads gradually became our dominant mode of off-road transportation. It would be a

---

[111] Uncle Bob offered us motorcycle advice and mechanical assistance until he died way too young of heart problems in 2002. When we put our own hillbilly trailer on the property in August of 1999, Bob's help was essential. One of my favorite times in the mountains was the New Year's Eve before the dreaded Y2K. Bob and his wife, Donnie, Paula's Grandma Bea, and Paula's sisters and their families joined us at the property. The weather was unusually balmy, and Bob set up his battery-powered TV next to our campfire circle so we could watch the world and Peter Jennings usher in the new millennium. I'm glad to have known Bob, and I miss his company, especially at the property.

few years before I went over to the quad side, but they began to appear in the family because the employer of Bob's wife, Donnie, was a big farming outfit, and they sold off quads after their workers had trashed them for a few years. Most of these quads were early Polaris 250 two-strokes. In retrospect, these ATVs from the early nineties seem crude compared to quads today, but Bob bought one and Warren bought two (plus one old Honda) from the farming company. Warren has his own twenty-acre walnut orchard, so the quads were put to use there. He also bought his kids a little 1989 Yamaha Breeze.

Eventually, Paula's step-dad, Ed, bought one of the Polaris quads from Warren because Warren had begun to upgrade. Ed suggested that I take his old dirtbike since he didn't need or want it any more. I really appreciated the offer. After all, how often can you get a bike for the cost of transferring the registration? The only problem was that the bike was an early 1970s Honda 125. And even though it was a neat old enduro, it was not really enough bike for a big boy like me. I rode it for a short time, but when it started having trouble I wasn't too interested in keeping it running. I parked it beside my garage, where it stayed until Uncle Warren decided he would take it and restore it for his daughter, Heather.

About the same time, we bought the little 1989 Yamaha Breeze for $900 from Warren, so that Paula would have something to ride. By the time we bought the Breeze, it had been ridden by every living person in the family. And it kept on chugging for us—long enough for it to be a reliable ride for our kids.[112] So for a brief time we had the Breeze and the old Honda bike. But the Honda gave out, and I was back to borrowing other rides.

Fortunately, Uncle Warren is always looking for a project, and he created a new, old bike out of the remains of two different vehicles: a Kawasaki dirtbike and a Honda ATC three-wheeler. Warren mounted the 185-cc ATC engine and transmission on the dirtbike frame. The result, which we called the Honduki, was a dirtbike that started (rope pull) and shifted (no clutch, neutral at the top) like an old three-wheeler. It also had an ATV thumb throttle. Warren's objective was to make the ultimate hill-climbing machine. Although the 185-cc engine didn't produce an abundance of power, the transmission was extremely low-geared (especially compared to typical dirtbikes) and, because it was clutchless, it was very difficult to stall it out. What this means is that the Honduki could literally walk up a hill, even Black Mountain.

Black Mountain is a fire service trail up a steep hill that was cut many years ago but has not been maintained for a long time. When I had my old Kawasaki, I tried so many times to climb Black Mountain. And I usually made it about ¾ of the way up the hill. At

---

[112] In the spring of 2006, seventeen years after it was manufactured, I sold the Breeze (for $500) back to Uncle Warren, who promptly rebuilt the top end. Though it has needed a starter for maybe two years, it runs pretty well once it gets going. I sold the old Breeze to Warren because we replaced it with a 2002 Yamaha Breeze.

that point on the hill, the "trail" forks a bit. To the left it's hard to maintain traction as you sidehill for a bit and then try to shoot the last and steepest section. On the Kawasaki, I could never get in position to go to the left, so I usually stayed on the right, which was really straight. Straight led the rider to a rock ledge that had to be climbed or jumped. You have to understand that when the bike hit the ledge it was already moving at an incredibly steep angle, and the ledge shot the front wheel even higher. If I got out of shape at all as I popped over the ledge, I had to let off the throttle for an instant, which would cost the old Kawasaki 175 too much momentum.

Warren has climbed Black Mountain on various bikes, and Bob did it in the old days. Ritch, my brother-in-law, climbed it once on the TT 500. Even my dad, who's only been to the property a few times, climbed it on his Polaris Sportsman 500 ATV (which is now Paula's ride). But I never made it. I have seen the crest, though, from the seat of the Honduki. I made it through the ruts and over the rocks to the fork near the top. I decided to go left, and I made the swing and got the bike headed straight for the last twenty feet. That's when the back wheel started spinning in loose soil. I lost traction and momentum and finally my balance. That was my last good run at Black Mountain. I now have a 4X4 ATV that could probably make it up the hill, but I don't like the idea of turning around a 500lb. quad on the side of a steep, rocky slope. I also don't want to flip a 500lb. quad on myself.

The Honduki was another one of those bikes that took some finesse and strength to start and ride. The pull start was unreliable, so pushing or rolling was the best option. But without a clutch, the transmission had to be tricked. Like the TT 500, the Honduki had a compression release on it, and to roll start it the rider pulled the lever while holding the gear shifter between first and second gear (not always easy). When enough speed had been attained, the compression release lever was released and the shifter shifted up to second gear. Did I mention that once the Honduki was running, the rider had to reach under the tank to turn off the choke—without taking it out of gear or letting off the throttle completely.

I got a kick out of riding the Honduki until I broke my toe on it. One fine spring weekend when most of the family was at the property, Warren and I decided to cut a new trail through some rough terrain. The new trail would actually connect two main trails by running down a hillside through bushes and around trees into a seasonal creek and then up another hill to meet up with a trail we call the "Pump Trail." It was hot, dirty work and I was just wearing a T-shirt, jeans, and tennis shoes. As soon as we finished clearing the trail, we went back to get bikes to run it. I hopped on the Honduki, got it started, and headed down the trail. When I reached the creek, I saw that I needed to thread my tires between some rocks. But I misjudged how low the foot pegs were on the Honduki and how tall the rocks were. I thought everything was cool as I negotiated my way between the rocks and started focusing on getting through the creek and up the other side. And then—BAM! My right foot, which was firmly on the peg, smashed into a rock. The peg didn't give and neither did the rock, so my toe did. It hurt; it swelled; we went home.

Part 3: The Trail Less Ridden

By about 2000, the quad revolution in the family had gained momentum. At that point Paula and I just had the old Breeze. I began to talk to my dad, who lives in Washington, about quads. As Christmas 2000 approached, we talked about him getting the girls either an off-road go-cart or a quad. Then my dad visited the local Polaris dealership, the owner of which was a regular customer at his auto repair shop, and he came home with a 90-cc Polaris kids' quad—and a Sportsman 500 for himself. Grandpa brought the kids their quad from Washington just after Christmas, but I had to wait almost a year before I finally got my own four-wheeler.[113]

---

[113] The kids were just four and six when they got their quad. Their birthdays are right after Christmas, though, so basically they started riding at five and seven. Our Abigail was the youngest kid in the family to ride by herself. I should point out here that the Consumer Product Safety Commission, which is not particularly fond of ATVs in general, has set out strict age guidelines for which size ATVs are appropriate for what ages. These guidelines only take into consideration engine size and child age. I have never put my daughters on quads they could not handle. But according to the guidelines, my ten-year-old, Abigail, isn't even ready for a 90-cc quad. She's supposed to be on a 50-cc. She'd look like a Shriner on a toy car. In fact, she's already too tall and too skilled for a stock 90-cc quad.

In September of 2001, my dad called to say that the luxury car dealer next to his repair shop had taken a quad in trade as part of a sale of a Porsche. Apparently, no one at the car dealer knew what to do with this quad, and the salesman who made the deal was on the hook until he got rid of it. At first, my dad didn't know the make and model of the quad. But then he called me back and said it was a 2000 Yamaha Kodiak and we could get it for around $3,000, and I said I would take it. I told him not to let anyone else get near it. I really didn't have the three grand and I didn't know where I would get it, but a new Kodiak, even in 2000, was almost $6,000. When the time came to pay, I gave the car dealer the number of my hardworking credit card. Then I had to wait for my dad to bring the ATV to California.

Our plan was for him to come to California (around the time of my birthday in October) in his motor home with my quad, his quad, and a friend's two quads on a trailer. He would come to Modesto, and the kids and I would join him on a trip down to the sand dunes at Pismo. We would be joined by my dad's cousin, Helmut (that's right, Helmut) and his wife Maryann, who would travel down in their own motor home. While he was in California, my dad needed to visit his mother, my grandmother, and help her with her affairs. And then for some reason known only to my dad and Satan, he decided to take Oma, as we sometimes call my grandmother, along for the trip to Pismo. Somehow, I just knew it was a bad idea to take a grumpy eighty-year-old German woman camping, and something also told me that this same grumpy eighty-year-old wouldn't have a fun time at the dunes. But it was too late for the kids and I to back out (Paula already had some excuse for not going.).

Before I go any farther, I need to point out that my dad and I had not been to Pismo in more than twenty years. Obviously, that means I was just a kid when we were last there. In the old days, our family went to Pismo a number of times with the Jeep club. I have two Pismo memories from childhood that stand out. First, one time we went to Pismo with our camp trailer expecting to camp on the beach with the rest of the Jeep club. However, when we arrived we discovered that there was a fierce wind blowing (hardly uncommon at Pismo) and the Jeep clubbers decided to camp far inland—where the dunes would offer some shelter from the winds. In order to get our trailer to the new camping spot, one of the other Jeepers hooked up his hot rod Jeep, equipped with a big V8 engine, headers, and paddles tires, to our trailer and hit the gas. The other jeeper, named Jim, pulled our trailer the length of what is called "the sand highway" (a trip of several miles) and parked it near Oso Flaco Lake and the Boy Scout Camp, which are now off-limits to off-roaders. The other memory I have, which may have occurred on the same trip as the other memory, was the time one of the less stable wives in the Jeep club got drunk and mad at her husband, and she took off into the dunes in their Jeep at night. She didn't just get lost; she ended up at the bottom of a sand bowl and couldn't get herself out. It took the men of the club most of the night to find her and get her Jeep safely out of the bowl.

In the intervening years between our visits, Pismo had changed a great deal. In the old days, the Pismo riding area covered over 12,000 acres of sand. Twenty years later, because of environmentalists (don't get me wrong, I love the environment) and developers, the area is down to less than 1,500 acres. We knew things would be different, but we didn't realize that now the riding area can only be accessed by driving at least one mile down the beach from the entrance on Pier Avenue. In other words, to ride quads or other off-road vehicles at Pismo, which is now called Oceano Dunes, you have to enter the beach at the ranger booth at the end of either Pier Avenue or Grand Avenue (which is one mile farther north from Pier) and then truck or trailer your bikes one mile (two miles if you enter at Grand) south on the beach until you reach the designated riding area.[114] You then unload on the sand, and then finally you go ride. The other option is to camp on the beach, or

---

[114] This trip down the beach is often complicated by the always-changing tide. When the tide is out just about any vehicle can make it across the wet, packed sand. When the tide is in, you better have four-wheel drive because you are going to be driving in the soft sand above the beach. Oh yeah, I forgot to mention, there's a small river, Arroyo Grande Creek, that cuts down across the beach, and you have to cross it to get to the riding area.

rather above the beach, in the riding area. Again, we didn't know any of this information before we got to Pismo.[115]

On a Friday afternoon, we pulled the motor homes into a campground that was practically adjacent to the beach entrance. We walked down to the ranger booth and learned that we would have to pull the quads on the trailer down the beach with the motor home.[116] This news created a bit of an inconvenience, but I was ready to ride my new quad. I suggested that we give it a shot while there was still some good daylight left. But the old folks thought it best to finish setting up camp and start cooking dinner. I pointed out that Jose's Cantina was right across the street, so we didn't need to cook an elaborate dinner. I was outvoted. The girls and I went for a swim in the campground's pool, and I spent most of the evening looking at my new quad on the trailer. The next morning, we missed low tide (when going down the beach is easier) because breakfast, which Oma insisted on cooking, took two or three hours to cook, eat, and clean up. Then we had to break camp a bit to get the motor home ready to drive down the beach. We finally reached the riding area by early afternoon on Saturday.

My Kodiak 400 is not exactly a dune machine. It is what is called a utility quad, which means it is more at home on the trails and hills, in mudbogs, and on the farm. Nevertheless, I enjoyed

---

[115] The term "Schmidt intelligence" may be an oxymoron.
[116] This was the first of several instances on this trip when I asked myself why I didn't drive my own pickup truck to Pismo.

getting used to it on the dunes that Saturday afternoon.[117] I found that as long as I could get a good run at a dune, I could probably make it to the top. I took the kids out for some short rides. And Helmut, Ernie (my dad), and I had a nice ride where we traded around on the quads. One of the quads Ernie borrowed from his friend was a new Yamaha Raptor, a powerful sport quad. On the Raptor, I raced up one hill and jumped over the crest. In the words of Napoleon Dynamite, I got "like three feet of air." Fortunately, I didn't wreck the quad like Napoleon's granny. After about three hours in the dunes, I was informed that Oma had had enough and it was time to go back to the campground to begin the hours-long preparation of dinner (apparently Jose's was out of the question again). As we left the dunes on Saturday afternoon, the kids and I held out hope that we would come out in the morning to ride before we began the long ride back to Modesto. Unfortunately, this trip would go down in our riding history as the three-day, three hours of riding fiasco. The fact that for all three days the temperature was in the mid-eighties, even at the beach, made everything more frustrating. I've been to Pismo four times since the 2001 trip, and I've never experienced weather like that again (of course, I haven't been able to go in the fall again, either.) To be fair to my dad, he is

---

[117] I have since ridden my Kodiak in the dunes many, many times, and I have always had a good time, and I've always been satisfied with its capabilities. On a subsequent trip to Pismo, I out-raced Uncle Warren up a dune (he was on a Honda Foreman 450). When I came down the hill, I hollered at him, "I thank God he gave me the good sense to ride a Yamaha!" Warren later bought my Yamaha.

usually much more enthusiastic about riding. In fact, he's a sixty-four-year-old near maniac on a quad. He has given my kids the opportunity to see him wipeout in the dunes at Florence, Oregon, which, by the way, is one of the most wonderful places in the world to ride and relax in general.

* * *

My kids will tell anyone who asks that their two favorite vacation spots are Disneyland and Florence, Oregon. They like Oregon because it is breathtakingly beautiful. I love the drive from I-5 over to the coast. There are a number of routes (none is fast) from which to choose, depending on what part of the coast you are going to visit. We usually turn off I-5 at Sutherlin and take Route 138 to Elkton, where we turn on to Route 38, which we follow to Reedsport on the coast. The landscape on this route varies between rolling pastures, thick evergreen forests, the scenic Umpqua River, and several quaint little towns. The road twists and turns for most of the way to the coast, and it can be a little treacherous in inclement weather, especially at night. Just a few miles from Reedsport, there is an elk preserve, with an elk viewing station along the south side of the highway (it also serves as a rest stop). The first time we passed by the elk viewing station, I saw the "Elk Viewing Station" sign on the road and looked to the huge meadow and marsh area that spreads out in front of the lookout. I said, "Elk viewing station? I don't see any. . .ELK! Holy cow, look at all those huge elks just lying out in the meadow!"[118]

When we get to Reedsport, we turn north on Highway 101 and drive along the coast for about twenty miles to Florence, which sits at the northern end of the forty-mile stretch of sand dunes that make up the Oregon Dunes National Recreation Area. Actually, the drive from Reedsport to Florence isn't technically along the coast. The highway runs behind the dunes that stand between the ocean and the coastal forests. In some places, the dunes reach more than two miles inland. Between 2001 and 2006, we visited Florence five times—once for Memorial Weekend, twice for weeklong vacations, once during the Holidays, and once at Easter. We have stayed in motels (there's a good Best Western maybe ½ mile from the dunes), rented vacation homes, and camped in our trailer. We've seen rain, hail (lightning and thunder), fog, and, actually, a lot of sunshine. We have met my dad there several times. We've traveled to Florence with friends and family from California. In 2003, we led a delegation of ten adults and ten children (all Paula's family), spreading the clan out in two rental houses. It hasn't always been easy, but we've always had fun.

Our girls love Florence because the town's historic downtown area is full of little shops that they are happy to visit and

---

[118] Dan Schmidt: master of the obvious!

re-visit. They also like that the Florence area dunes offer plenty of easy to ride space for them to have fun on their quads. As far as I can tell, Paula enjoys Florence because when she tires of riding, civilization is only a few minutes away, and there are many other things to do in the area. The Florence riding experience (along with the other Oregon dune areas) really can't be matched anywhere else. The two words that really describe the Florence riding area are "space" and "variety." The sand covers around 12,000 acres in Florence, and there is a seven-mile stretch of beach open to riding. But in Florence, you don't just find a beach and some dunes. Just up from the beach, running the whole seven-mile stretch, is a line of small but tricky and often steep dunes that are rimmed with vegetation. Inland from these dunes, there is a large area of fairly dense vegetation, where you find only a few sand trails and roads. There are more trails at the inland edge of the bush area. These twisty trails are great fun for games of follow-the-leader. Then the area opens up to a tremendous open expanse of sand. At the northern end is the wide open and mostly flat Goose Pasture (where the kids like to ride), and to the south are the big dunes, with names like Competition Hill, and steep bowls. Perhaps the coolest riding in Florence, though, is found even farther inland, where the sand stretches into the pine forests. Riding on sand through a forest on a tight trail with high-bermed corners is an absolute blast and it's quite unique. And you never know when the trail you are riding is going to dead-end into a pristine freshwater lake. That's when it's nice to be riding a quad with a reverse gear.

    No matter where you go on the dunes at Florence you'll find an incredible view. All you have to do is climb the hill that's just across from the South Jetty parking lot and turn around at the top. You'll see the Siuslaw River snaking its way north and out to the Pacific. If you make it to the top of one of the big dunes out in the open area, you'll be able to see miles of coastline, sand, and forest. I need to finish this section on Florence because I would rather be riding there than writing here. I can't leave Oregon without mentioning Jessie M. Honeyman State Park, which borders the dune area just south of Florence. The park features a huge, scenic campground with hundreds of camping spaces that are often booked months in advance (if you want a good space during the summer, you better reserve it by February). Besides the campground, the park's major attraction is Cleawox Lake. Cleawox Lake is a freshwater lake surrounded by pine trees and sand dunes. The beaches around the lake are actually made up of beach sand. The western edge of the lake is a sand dune that comes down all the way to the water, and kids slide down this dune on sand boards. Others just tumble down the dune and plop into the water. The lake is open to swimming, fishing, and rowing, and there is an old store/ranger office, made of stone and wood, that was once the local headquarters of the Conservation Corps, who built the park and campground in the 1930s. To me, Honeyman embodies a kind of classic American vacation ideal (which, I admit, has been influenced by the movies), and I am grateful that my family has been able to experience it.

I am thankful, too, that we continue to enjoy the family property. I don't know if I have ever been happier than those times when the four of us (Paula, Emily, Abigail, and your Author) have ridden one after the other down one of our favorite trails. Admittedly, the property is about three rungs on the ladder below rustic, and we've been victimized by vandals (both human and bear) in recent years—which doesn't help. More troubling to me is the fact that our lives keep getting busier and more complicated, which leaves less time to run off to the hills for the weekend. Work, school, sports, and church keep us off the trails more often than I would like. But sometimes it's just the hope of riding that gets me through the tired class, boring meeting, etc. When the fall semester (for instance) starts to drag, I focus on the Thanksgiving weekend that I know will eventually come. And I think about the kids playing and riding their quads around the track, down in our meadow, where they learned to ride—where I learned to ride.

www.ingramcontent.com/pod-product-compliance
Lightning Source LLC
LaVergne TN
LVHW011419080426
835512LV00005B/157